Favorite
Helpful
Hints

Cover Design: Jeff Hapner
Illustrations: Ilene Berg

ISBN: 0-88176-297-0

Printed in Canada

Contents

All About
This Book

Chances are that you, like most people, are a creature of habit, especially when it comes to the routine responsibilities and chores that you carry out, most of the time, without giving them more thought than absolutely necessary. Washing windows, after all, is not an inspiring task. You have to do it, but no one says you have to enjoy it. And the end result of waxing the floor may be pleasing, but wouldn't it be gratifying if there were a faster, easier way to do it? Maybe there is. And that's what this book is all about.

Favorite Helpful Hints brings together hundreds of great hints for making your life run more smoothly and for making the way you handle everyday chores easier, speedier, more efficient, or more economical. Every area of caring for your home is covered, from keeping the house safe to finding extra storage space in the garage, from do-it-yourself maintenance and repairs to plumbing, electricity, pest control, and energy-saving.

The first chapter, "Hints for a Well-Organized Home," contains a terrific assortment of tips on keeping your household running smoothly—from making the most of your storage space (and there are some really innovative ideas here) to planning your activities to correspond to your personal energy-level pattern.

An important chapter on home safety follows. "Keeping Your Home Safe" offers valuable hints on how to identify and correct potential hazards in your home.

"Cleaning Around the Home" is a fascinating collection of clever and unusual tips on every aspect of your home-cleaning chores. "General Home Maintenance" offers tips designed to help you keep your home in good shape, and save money by performing necessary repairs yourself. Home maintenance is also the subject of the following two chapters. "Painting and Decorating" has dozens of tips for the do-it-yourselfer, covering such topics as buying, using, and storing paint, choosing and using tools, and tackling tricky repairs. "Outside Home Repairs" deals with roof repairs and outdoor maintenance, and offers tips on other outdoor projects. It gives more advice on tools and safe use of a ladder too.

The following chapter has terrific ideas for organizing and maintaining some of the most useful—and often underused—areas of your home. "Workshop, Basement, and Garage" has any number of space- and time-saving tips, hints for easy cleanup, and advice for woodworkers.

Both ecologically and economically, energy conservation is a major issue these days. Learn how you can help protect the environment and cut back on your utility bills from the chapter "Saving Energy in the Home."

Favorite Helpful Hints has been organized to make it as easy as possible for you to find the information you're looking for as quickly as possible.

One thing you can be sure of—anywhere you look you'll find the sort of terrific idea that makes you exclaim, "Now, why didn't *I* think of that?"

Hints for a Well-Organized Home

Keeping the Household Running Smoothly

When lining garbage cans with plastic trash bags, nest several bags into a can at the same time. Then remove the bags, one by one, as they fill.

Decide on the time of day when your energy level is highest and do your least favorite chore then. You'll find you can get through it much more easily. Wind down the day with one of your favorite things, no matter how simple.

Kids can help you get the day going by making their own lunches. While you get breakfast, the kids can make sandwiches with lunch meats and spreads left ready to use on a tray in the refrigerator.

If you have trouble getting started in the morning, get organized the night before. Lay out your clothes, measure the coffee, and set the breakfast table before you go to bed.

Pin the menus for the week on a bulletin board—with the recipe titles and cookbook page references—for everyone in the family to see. The first one home can start the meal.

To save time and energy at the grocery store, make out your shopping list in the same order as the food is stocked in the store aisles.

Assign a color to each family member and color code items throughout the house. Schoolbags, umbrellas, ponchos, coat hooks, storage boxes, and lunchboxes can all be color coded this way.

Add shelves above your washer and dryer to hold colored plastic baskets—one color for each family member. When you take clean clothes out of the dryer, sort each person's clothes into the appropriate basket. Family members can then pick up their baskets and fold and put away their own clothes.

Instead of using an address book, keep a record of names and addresses on index cards stored in a file box. If someone moves, just substitute a new card with the current information. This method also gives you more space for records of birthdays, anniversaries, and clothing sizes.

Designate one area of your home, even if it's only one drawer somewhere, for filing business papers, bills, letters, and clippings.

Use the back of junk mail letters and envelopes for shopping lists or telephone messages.

Organize your records by category with the help of stick-on colored dots. All your classical records can be coded with one color, rock music with another, musicals with another, and so on.

The instruction booklets that come with appliances won't be so easily misplaced if you keep them handy in a notebook. Paste the back cover of each booklet against one of the notebook's three-hole-punched sheets, and you'll know just where to find the information when you need it. The same goes for household documents, mortgage agreements, insurance policies, and so on.

Organization and Storage

If your home is built with studs and drywall, you can add cabinets between the studs, anywhere you need them—they won't take up any space at all. For example, put a liquor cabinet over your bar, or fashion a canned-goods pantry in your kitchen.

Pegboard is most often used on walls, but it can also be used as a room divider, or even to make the inside of a closet or cabinet door more functional. When installing pegboard, remember to provide space behind the panels for the hooks.

If you're short on wall space for books, you can pull a sofa away from a wall and surround it with arm-height bookcases.

Glass baby food jars are ideal for storing nails and screws. Better yet, nail the caps to a wood base or wall plaque, and just screw the jars into place. And remember that partly used tubes of glue won't dry out if they're kept in a tightly closed jar.

Use flat, roll-out bins for under-the-bed storage. They can hold bed linens, sewing supplies, and infrequently used items.

Nail coffee cans to the wall to make bins for clips, pins, or other small items.

To increase the capacity and efficiency of a drawer, outfit it with a lift-out tray. Fill the tray with items you frequently use, and use the space beneath the tray for articles you seldom need.

Add more storage space in your bedroom by building a headboard storage unit. You can place books, lamps, or a radio on the lid of the unit and inside you can store extra linens and blankets.

For extra closet storage, see if your closets can accommodate a second shelf above the existing one. And if you install the main clothes-hanging rod high enough, you may be able to install another rod beneath it on which to hang shorter items such as slacks and shirts.

Put the space under a stairway to work as a storage area. Construct a wheeled, wedge-shaped container that fits into the farthest area beneath the steps.

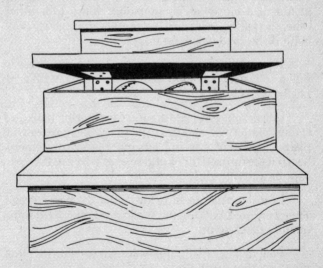

Another way to use a stairway as a storage area is to replace ordinary nailed-in-place steps with hinged steps. Use the space under the hinged steps to hold boots or sports equipment.

Hooks, shelves, or hanging bins can transform the inside surfaces of closet doors into useful storage areas.

If your cedar chest or closet no longer smells of cedar, lightly sand its surfaces. Sanding opens the wood's pores and releases a fresh cedar scent. Remember that the scent doesn't kill moths; it merely repels them. So, it's best to clean all clothes before storing to remove any moth eggs.

Convert an ordinary closet or chest into a cedar closet or chest by installing thin cedar slats over inside surfaces. Then weatherstrip to contain the scent.

Install two rows of clothing and coat hooks on your closet doors—one down low for a child to use, another higher up for you to use.

If you color code cups and toothbrushes in the bathroom—with each family member choosing a different color—there'll be no confusion over what belongs to each person.

So that you won't misplace frequently used items, glue small magnets on the walls of the medicine cabinet to hold nail files, cuticle scissors, clippers, and other small metal objects.

Hang a basket near the front door and keep your keys in it, so you'll always know where they are. Use this basket also for bills and letters that need to be mailed. When you grab your keys, you'll remember to pick up the mail as well.

Extension cords won't get tangled when stored in a drawer if you wind them and secure them with rubber bands—or slip them into a toilet paper or paper towel tube.

To keep a broom from resting on its bristles and thus becoming lopsided, drill a hole in the broom's handle and hang the broom on the wall.

Keep flashlight batteries fresh by storing them in a sealed plastic bag in the refrigerator.

When storing suitcases, put an unwrapped cake of soap inside each one to prevent musty odors from developing.

To give yourself more storage space in a small bathroom, erect shelves in the "dead" wall space beside the vanity, over the toilet, or behind the door. Such shelves offer convenient storage without intruding on floor space.

Make your shower curtain rod do double duty—attach extra curtain hooks to hold a back brush, a net bag for bath toys, each family member's washcloth, or a shower cap.

Keep place mats flat and out of the way by hanging them on a clipboard hung from a hook inside a cabinet or pantry door.

Keep your wet umbrella in the shower where it can drip away without making a mess. This is an especially useful strategy when you have company on a rainy day, and everyone has an umbrella.

You'll always know where your photo negatives are if you store them behind corresponding prints in your photo album.

Photographic film will stay fresh longer if stored in your refrigerator.

Moving House

Moving will go more smoothly if you make a master checklist of everything that must be done in connection with the move. So that you don't fall behind, schedule a deadline for each task.

When notifying people about your move, be sure to include utilities, post office, social security, publications to which you subscribe, doctors, insurance companies, and the phone company. If you also go through your address book, you'll be less likely to overlook someone who'll want or need to know you're moving.

Take a survival package along with the family so you can camp in your new home until the moving van arrives. Include instant coffee, cups, spoons, soap and towels, a can and bottle opener, some light bulbs, a flashlight, toilet paper, cleansing powder, and a first aid kit. Also be sure that daily medications travel with you.

To prevent odors from developing in the refrigerator or freezer during the move, put several charcoal briquettes inside the unit to absorb the odors. Or fill the refrigerator or freezer with wadded-up newspapers. The paper will absorb any moisture and help prevent odors.

If you're going to move a considerable distance, get your youngsters into the act. Encourage them to look up facts on your new location at the library, and let them help you plot the most convenient route on a map. If you're moving only a short distance, let them examine the new house and neighborhood before the move.

When leaving your previous home, empty the children's rooms last, and restructure their rooms first when you've arrived at your new home. This helps them adjust psychologically.

If you hold a house or garage sale to dispose of unwanted items before moving, you'll not only make money, you'll save money by not having to pay for transporting unwanted possessions.

To keep pairs of shoes together, tie them with yarn or string.

To get the best prices at your moving sale, clean and shine the objects you're selling—and display them creatively.

Your sale will be more organized if you categorize odds and ends in bins. For example, have one bin for kitchen gadgets, another for books, and another for records.

To display the clothes you're selling, rig up a clothesline. You can also throw an old sheet over part of the clothesline for a makeshift dressing room.

Make sure you have plenty of newspapers, old boxes, and grocery bags for packing up the items purchased.

Save space by not packing the unbreakable contents of tightly loaded drawers. Simply tape the drawers in place with strips of wide masking tape. To minimize tape marks, remove the tape as soon as the furniture arrives at your new home.

Get carpets and slipcovers cleaned before you move. They'll come back wrapped and ready to go.

Small linens such as towels, washcloths, and pillowcases also can serve as packing material for dishes and glassware—and they don't waste space.

If you pack books so their spines are alternated, they will take up less space. (It may be cheaper to ship books via the United States mail, since the post office offers an inexpensive, fourth-class book rate.)

Plates are less likely to break if they are packed standing on edge. To minimize breakage of glass items, place the heavier ones on the bottom and the more delicate ones on top. Excelsior or pieces of crumpled newspaper make good packing material. If you have several days to pack before moving, dampen the excelsior so it will shape itself to the china and glassware.

Because furniture casters sometimes fall out when a piece is lifted, remove them ahead of time. Tie them together with heavy twine, and tag them so you know which piece of furniture they fit.

As you tape up each packed box, place a piece of kite string underneath the tape, leaving about an inch sticking out. When it's time to unpack, just pull on the string, which will slit right through the tape.

If you have access to the new home a day or so before the van arrives, you could set off a bug bomb or spray. (Even if you don't see bugs, there may be some.) This way, you won't worry about your family, your pets, foods, or furnishings during the spraying.

If you're going to arrive before the movers, consider bringing a book, radio, or portable television with you to while away the wait.

To save time and eliminate confusion when the movers arrive, draw a floor plan of your new home ahead of time. Sketch in and number your furnishings the way you want them arranged. Tag furniture pieces to correspond to the floor plan so the movers know where to put each piece.

If you drive to your new location and arrive late, spend the first night at a motel rather than trying to "settle in" when everyone's tired. Everything will seem much more manageable in the morning.

Keeping Your Home Safe

Preventing Accidents in the Home

To avoid accidents, wipe up spilled water, grease, and other liquids from your kitchen, bathroom, and garage floors as soon as possible.

Anchor rolled up sections of carpet firmly to prevent someone from tripping.

Secure throw rugs with nonskid pads and don't use them at the top or bottom of a flight of stairs.

If your basement stairs are to be painted, add a little sand to the paint for a better grip, or install rubber or abrasive treads.

If you staple burlap to the bottom step of a ladder, you'll have a scraper for your shoes. This way you won't have any slippery substances left on your shoes.

To prevent grease fires, keep the stove clear of pot holders, paper napkins, and towels when frying food.

Keep baking powder on hand for extinguishing a kitchen fire in an emergency.

Don't put hot tea, coffee, or other hot liquids on a table cloth that hangs way over the side of the table. Someone could trip on the cloth and spill the scalding liquid.

Keep the gas cooktop away from open windows where curtains could blow into the flames or where wind could extinguish the cooking flames.

When handing a knife to someone else, always hold the point turned away from the other person.

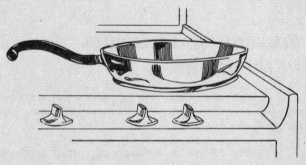

Keep the handles of pots and frying pans turned inward on the kitchen range so that they cannot be knocked or tipped over by accident. This is especially important if there are young children in the household.

Check all your child's toys to be sure any eyes, noses, knobs, or other parts will not come off when pulled or chewed.

Never leave a small child unattended in the bathtub.

In the bathtub, face your child toward the hot water faucet so he won't accidentally bump into the hot metal.

Don't hold a child on your lap while you drink or pass a hot beverage, or while you smoke.

Tie a bell around all bottles and containers that hold poisonous materials in the house to alert you to your child getting into something dangerous.

Store all your poisonous materials on high shelves, out of the reach of children. And remember to label the containers.

Some poison control centers supply stickers to put on dangerous chemicals so that a child understands that they are harmful. Ask if these are available in your locality.

It's best never to place pillows in an infant's crib and to keep the crib completely away from the cord of a Venetian blind.

Never place a plastic bag or thin plastic covering within reach of an infant or small child, or near the child's bed.

Keep home workshop tools disconnected, and lock switches and power supplies so a child can't turn them on.

Fire Prevention and Safety

Assign a special closet to combustible materials and dangerous tools that you don't want your children to touch. Put a good lock on the door and a heat detector inside to alert you of any fire danger.

Every room in the house should have at least two escape exits.

If you have school-age children, make sure that the school carries out regular fire drills and that the children know where to go and what to do in case of fire.

Don't overload electrical circuits with too many appliances.

Replace frayed electrical cords before they burn or cause a fire.

Don't run extension cords under the rugs. The cords wear easily and may short out, causing a fire.

Keep combustibles away from the furnace, which can give off flames or sparks at times.

For basic protection at minimum expense, locate one smoke detector in the hallway near each separate sleeping area. (More complete protection calls for a detector on every level of a home.)

Remember that smoke detectors are unreliable below 40° F.

Some fire departments supply stickers that can be placed in a window to alert firefighters to the presence of a child or an elderly or handicapped person. Inquire if such stickers are available in your locality.

If you live or work in a high-rise building, locate the fire exits on your floor. If an alarm sounds, remember that you should always use the fire stairs, not the elevator.

Learn to distinguish the sound of a fire alarm in your building from the sound of an elevator alarm bell. If you think someone's trapped in the elevator when, in fact, the building is starting to go up in flames, you could be in serious trouble.

Walk your family through a fire drill so everyone knows what to do and where to go in case of fire. Make sure children know just where the family will reunite if they have to leave the house in case of fire.

Never use water on electric, oil, or grease fires. Water will only spatter the flames.

If you can't shut off the gas before fighting a gas fire, get out of the house immediately.

If you can't remove the fuel from a wood, paper, or fabric fire, cut off its air by smothering the fire with a coat or heavy woolen blanket. You might also cool the fire with water, a fire extinguisher, sand, or earth.

Distribute fire extinguishers in key areas such as the kitchen, bedrooms, workshop, and garage.

Never spend more than 30 seconds fighting a fire. If the fire can't be extinguished, warn others, get out of the house, and call the fire department.

Even if a fire is confined to a frying pan or wastebasket, never spend more than 30 seconds fighting the fire. Small fires can grow with frightening speed.

Never reenter a burning house for any reason. Leave fire fighting to the professionals as soon as they're on the scene.

Electrical and Storm Safety

Never place an electric appliance where it can fall in water.

Never touch an electric appliance while you are standing in water.

Don't place electric heaters near combustible materials.

As a safety precaution before leaving the house on vacation, unplug all electrical appliances except for those lights connected to automatic timers.

If you live in a storm-prone area, nail down roof shingles or use adequate adhesive to keep them from blowing off in a violent wind. For roofs with shingles that are not the seal-down type, apply a little dab of roofing cement under each tab.

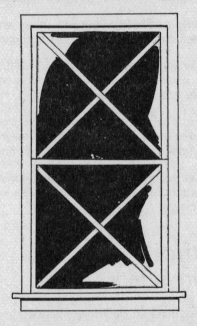

When a major storm is imminent, close shutters, board windows, or tape the inside of larger panes with an "X" along the full length of their diagonals. Even a light material like masking tape may give the glass the extra margin of strength it needs to resist cracking. Exception: When a tornado threatens, leave windows slightly ajar.

Alert your local police department if you discover downed power lines. Set up barricades to keep others away from the area until help arrives.

A lightning protection system should offer an easy, direct path for the bolt to follow into the ground and thus prevent injury or damage while the bolt is traveling that path.

Grounding rods (at least two for a small house) should be placed at opposite corners of the house.

Keep an eye on large trees—even healthy ones—that could damage your house if felled in a storm. Cut them back if necessary.

Store a lantern, pick, shovel, crowbar, hammer, screwdriver, and pliers in your storm shelter. If the exit becomes blocked you may have to dig your way out. Store canned food and bottled water, too.

The basement is not a good shelter during a tornado because it's too close to gas pipes, sewer pipes, drains, and cesspool. A better shelter would be underground, far from the house (in case the roof falls) and away from the gas and sewer system.

In a hurricane, don't go out unless you have to. However, if flooding threatens, seek high ground and follow the instructions of civil defense personnel.

A spare tire in the trunk of your car can be used as a life preserver in a flooding or drowning emergency. Make sure the tire is in good shape.

Home and Personal Security

Plan to burgle yourself. In this game, you'll discover any weaknesses in your home protection system that may have previously escaped your notice.

Before turning your house key over to a professional housecleaner for several hours, make sure the person is honest and reputable as well as hard-working. Check all references thoroughly by telephone. If the housecleaner is from a firm, call your local Better Business Bureau to check on the firm's reputation. Make sure the firm insures its employees against accidents and theft.

Instead of keeping a spare key in a mailbox, under the door mat, or on a nail behind the garage, wrap the key in foil—or put it in a 35mm film can or a pipe tobacco can—and bury it where you can easily find it if you need it.

If your plans to be away from home have been publicized through a funeral, wedding, or similar newspaper notice, hire a house sitter. Burglars often read the newspapers to see who's planning to be away from home all day or for several days.

Dogs are among the best deterrents to burglars; even a small, noisy dog can be effective—burglars do not like to have attention drawn to their presence.

For the most effective alarm system, conceal all wiring. A burglar looks for places where he can disconnect the security system.

A door with too much space between the door and the frame is an invitation for the burglar to use a jimmy. Reinforce such a door by attaching a panel of ¾-inch plywood or a piece of sheet metal to it.

If there are door hinges on the outside of your house, take down the door and reset the hinges inside. Otherwise all a thief has to do to gain entry to your home is knock out the hinge pin.

You can burglar-proof your glass patio doors by setting a pipe or metal bar in the inside bottom track of the door slide. The pipe should be the same length as the track.

Ask for credentials from any salesman who requests entry to your home—even security system salesmen. Many professional burglars use this cover to check out homes. If you want to buy an electronic alarm system, make your own contacts with reputable firms.

Protect your windows with one or more good locks, an alarm system, burglar-resistant glass, or many small panes instead of one large area of glass.

When putting window locks on, have all the locks keyed alike and give each family member a key. Keep a key near the window where children can get it (but a burglar can't reach it) in case of fire.

After installing a window lock, drip some solder onto the screw heads. That will stop a burglar from unscrewing the lock after cutting a small hole in the window pane.

It can be a problem to lock an aluminum sliding window in a ventilating position. A locking sliding window bolt allows high security as it foils entry even if the glass is broken.

To help burglar-proof your home, install 1-inch throw deadbolt locks on all exterior doors.

A spring-latch lock is easy prey for burglars who are "loiding" experts. Loiding is the method of slipping a plastic credit card against the latch tongue to depress it and unlock the door. A deadbolt defies any such attack. It is only vulnerable when there is enough space between the door and its frame to allow an intruder to use power tools or a hacksaw. But using tools takes time—to the burglar's disadvantage.

When you move into a new house, it's a good idea to change all the locks and tumblers.

Change your lock cylinders from time to time, just in case someone has gotten hold of a set of your keys. If you lose your keys, change the cylinder immediately.

In a rented house, install a double cylinder lock that requires a key to open it from the inside as well as from the outside. If a thief breaks through the panel and reaches in, he still has the lock to deal with instead of just a knob.

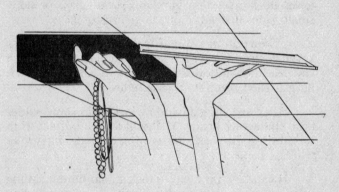

If you don't have a safe, or feel you don't need one, find good hiding places for your valuables in your home. An acoustical tile ceiling offers good hiding possibilities. Remove a tile and restore it afterwards with magnetic fastener or a similar device. However, be careful not to leave finger marks.

You can keep your jewelry safe by installing a wall-outlet safe. When the safe is closed, it looks just like an electrical outlet. When buying a wall safe, be sure it's fireproof as well as burglar-proof.

Are you worried about someone entering your house through your attached garage? If the garage door lifts on a track a C-clamp can provide extra security since the door cannot be opened if you tighten the C-clamp on the track next to the roller.

Another way to increase garage security is to install a peephole in the door separating the house from the garage. If you hear suspicious sounds, you can check without opening the door.

If you frost or cover your garage windows, burglars won't be able to tell if your car is gone.

Keep your garage door closed and locked even when your car is not in the garage.

When shopping, watch for pickpockets in places like the checkout counter where you normally lay down your purse or parcel. Also be alert at store entrances, on escalators and in elevators, in bargain areas, or in demonstration areas.

When shopping, it's best to carry a zippered shoulder bag with any outside pockets facing toward you. Don't carry large amounts of cash, and divide your cash among the purse, your eyeglasses case, and inner clothes pockets.

Cleaning Around The Home

General Cleaning Tips

The acid in vinegar makes it a good preventive wash for areas where mildew might form.

To remove discoloration from a yellowed bathtub, rub the tub with a solution of salt and turpentine.

So that you don't have to guess when trying to mix correct solutions of cleaning compounds, use red fingernail polish to plainly mark pint, quart, and gallon levels inside a bucket.

Dust and other debris often collect in hard-to-reach corners, such as behind large appliances, but you can reach easily into these corners with a yardstick. Make a yardstick "duster" by covering the end with a sock, secured with rubber bands, or by fastening a small sponge to the end of the yardstick with staples or rubber bands.

You can eliminate tiny scratches on glass by polishing the affected areas with toothpaste.

A portable blow dryer can soften wax that has dripped onto wooden surfaces. Wipe away the wax with a paper towel, then rinse the area with a mixture of vinegar and water. Dry thoroughly.

You can get stale odors out of sponges by washing them in the dishwasher, or by soaking them overnight in a bowl of bleach and rinsing them well the next morning.

Make an efficient cleaning apron from a compartmented shoe bag by attaching strings and filling the pockets with rags, polishes, brushes, and other lightweight supplies.

Old toothbrushes can be put to good use as hair dye applicators, or as cleaning brushes for silverware, combs, and typewriter keys.

To clean your radiators, hang a damp cloth behind the radiator, then blow on the radiator with a hair dryer to force hidden dirt and dust onto the damp cloth.

An automobile snow brush is perfect for cleaning under a refrigerator.

If you're tired of buying new dust mops because the old ones get dirty so quickly, cover your mop with an old nylon stocking. When the stocking gets soiled, simply discard it and replace it with another.

When a spray bottle's suction tube doesn't reach the liquid because most of the liquid has been used up, drop marbles or pebbles into the bottle until the level of the liquid rises enough to cover the end of the tube.

Want to dust furniture quick as a flash? Dampen two old cotton gloves or socks with furniture polish, slip them over your hands and then dust with both hands.

Worn-out cotton sweat socks—particularly those with terry-lined feet—make excellent dusting mitts.

Instead of buying dust cloths chemically treated to "attract" dust, make your own from cheesecloth. Dip the cloth in a solution of 2 cups of water and ¼ cup of lemon oil and allow it to dry before using.

Paint brushes make excellent dusters for small or hard-to-reach areas. Flick them along door jambs, around windows, and into corners.

To avoid snagging or harming delicate fabric when dusting ruffled or pleated lamp shades, use an old shaving brush or a baby's hair brush. The bristles are soft and effective.

You can use a straightened wire hanger to unclog a jammed vacuum cleaner hose. Leave a small hook at the end of the hanger and maneuver it back and forth; then, see if the hose is free of debris by dropping a coin through it. If the coin rolls out the other end, you're ready to vacuum again. If it doesn't, you'll have to maneuver the hanger some more. Another way to unclog a vacuum cleaner hose is to push an ordinary garden hose through it.

It's annoying to discover that the vacuum cord doesn't extend as far as you need it to. Rather than have to look for other wall sockets (usually located behind furniture), just add an extension to your cleaner's present cord.

To prevent a dust cloud from forming, empty a vacuum cleaner bag into a large plastic garbage bag; hold the mouth of the bag shut as you dump the dust inside it.

It's best to empty vacuum cleaner bags when they're about two-thirds full; a full bag reduces suction power.

Mend a torn reusable vacuum cleaner bag by pressing iron-on patches over the tears.

Cleaning Furniture and Household Objects

Leftover tea makes a good cleaning agent for varnished furniture.

Rub walnut or pecan meat over scratches in finished wood; the oil often hides them. Liquid shoe polish often covers scratches, too.

After polishing furniture, sprinkle on a little cornstarch and rub to a high gloss. Cornstarch absorbs oil and leaves a glistening, fingerprint-free surface.

Paste furniture wax or oil furniture polish will camouflage tiny furniture scratches.

To treat scratches on natural wood or antique finishes, polish with a mixture of equal amounts of turpentine and boiled linseed oil. Apply with a clean, soft, damp cloth.

Any scratch made by a match can be removed by rubbing it with a lemon wedge.

When cleaning picture glass, carefully dust the glass, and then polish it with tissues sold for cleaning eyeglasses. Avoid liquid cleaners because they could seep under the edge of the glass and spoil the photo or artwork. If you do use liquid cleaners, apply them to a cloth, *never* directly to the glass.

To make a tarnished gilt frame gleam again, wipe it with a rag dampened with turpentine.

To avoid damaging a picture or painting when polishing its wooden frame, spray the polish on a cloth, not on the frame, and then carefully apply to the frame.

To clean deeply carved picture frames, use a clean, dry, plastic squeeze bottle, pumping the bottle like a small bellows to blow dust from tiny crevices.

Valuables and Art Objects

To clean tarnished silver, place the items in a glass dish, add a piece of aluminum foil, and cover with a quart of hot water mixed with 1 tablespoon of baking soda. A reaction between the foil and the silver will remove any tarnish. Don't use this process on raised designs, however. You'll lose the dark accents of the sculpture.

An easy way to clean silver is with ordinary baking soda. Make a paste from 3 parts soda to 1 part water. Using a soft cloth, rub the paste gently on the silver surface. Tarnish will disappear rapidly. After rinsing, buff the silver with a soft cloth to bring up the shine.

To restore luster to a dried-out emerald or jade, dip a toothpick in olive oil and gently rub it over the stone's surface. (Use this method only if the piece won't be resold, since the stone may darken.)

An inexpensive way to clean gold is to mix 1 teaspoon of cigarette ash with enough water to form a paste. Rub the paste onto the surface of the gold with a soft cloth, rinse, and buff dry with a chamois. If no one in the house smokes, use baking soda instead of cigarette ash.

Always keep ivory objects where light can reach them, because steady darkness causes ivory to yellow.

To clean a yellowing ivory object, cut a lemon in half, dip it in salt, and rub it over the ivory surface. When the surface is dry, wipe it with a damp cloth, then buff dry for bright finish.

You can remove stubborn stains from ivory or plastic piano keys with a damp cloth dipped in baking soda, being careful not to let the soda fall between the keys. Wipe the keys off with another cloth, and buff them dry.

Cleaning Challenges

To keep vinyl and imitation leather-covered books looking good as new, wash them periodically with a mild detergent and then treat with a light coat of petroleum jelly or a vinyl dressing.

It is easy to clean lightly soiled records on the turntable. Gently hold a clean dust cloth on a record and allow the disc to turn at least three revolutions under the cloth. You'll be cleaning with the grooves, not across them, and so won't damage the record.

Treat leather-bound books periodically with a light oil so that the leather won't dry out and crack.

If you arrange books at the front of shelves, air will be able to circulate and prevent mustiness.

Protect books from direct sunlight, because it can fade the bindings and cause them to deteriorate.

In order to remove grease stains from books rub the affected areas with soft, white breadcrumbs.

Sprinkle damp book pages with talcum powder or cornstarch until the moisture is absorbed, then shake or brush the powder away.

Do you have black scuff marks on your luggage? They'll rub off with lemon extract.

Clean colored leather luggage with mild soapsuds and a damp sponge or soft-nap cloth.

The best way to clean regular leather luggage is to use a soft, clean rag to rub in a few drops of baby shampoo, a small area at a time. Repeat until all surfaces are covered. Use the same cloth to buff the luggage to a natural sheen.

Lampshades fixed to their frames with glue should be dry cleaned.

When lampshades aren't glued to their frames, wash them in the bathtub with warm water and a spray hose. Dry them quickly after washing so the frames won't rust. An electric fan or hair dryer can speed the drying process.

To keep a phone clean and germfree, rub it with an alcohol-soaked paper towel.

To wash fragile objects without breaking them, put them on a tray in the sink and spray them first with window cleaner or foam bathroom cleaner, and then with water. Let them air dry on a towel.

You can wash knickknacks more quickly than you can dust them. Swish them in water containing a touch of liquid detergent, rinse, and drain on a towel. If you want to make sure every crevice is dry, use a hair dryer.

Remove traces of rust on iron by rubbing with an emery cloth, or with steel wool moistened with a few drops of turpentine or kerosene.

It is possible to clean a chandelier without taking it down; here's how. In a glass, mix a solution of 1 part denatured alcohol and 3 parts water. Cover the floor or table under the chandelier with newspaper or plastic and set up a ladder so that you can reach the fixture's pendants. Individually submerge the crystals in the glass for a few moments, swishing them back and forth a little, and then simply let them air dry.

To get rid of stale cigarette or cigar smoke, leave a dish of vinegar or ammonia in the room overnight. It also helps to dampen a towel with diluted vinegar and wave it through the room.

Clean and sweeten ashtrays by washing them in a solution of 1 tablespoon of baking soda to a quart of water.

If candle wax has dripped on a table or cloth, hold

an ice cube against the wax until it's brittle, and then pry it off with a knife or your fingernail.

If silver candlesticks accumulate wax drippings, place them in the freezer; when the wax freezes, you'll be able to peel it off.

To make a copper/brass/bronze cleaner, stir together 1 tablespoon of table salt and 1 tablespoon of flour. Continuing to stir, add 1 tablespoon of white vinegar. Apply the resulting paste with a damp cloth or sponge, rub gently, then rinse and wipe dry.

Sometimes a slightly tarnished aluminum surface can be cleaned by rubbing it with crumpled aluminum foil.

Fireplace smoke stains can be removed by washing them with ½ cup of trisodium phosphate (TSP) mixed in 1 gallon of water. (Wear gloves to protect your hands.) You also can remove fireplace smoke stains by rubbing them with an art gum eraser, or by applying a paste of cream of tartar and water; when the paste dries brush it off, along with the stains.

Cleaning and Waxing Floors

A mopped floor occasionally dries with a luster-dulling film; if you mop it again with water containing a cup or so of white vinegar the floor will glisten.

A pencil eraser or fine, dry steel wool is often effective in removing scuff marks left by shoe heels on resilient flooring. Lift crayon marks by rubbing them with toothpaste or silver polish on a damp rag.

Instead of using commercial preparations, you can "wax" a floor by washing it with warm water to which you have added 2 tablespoons of furniture polish and ½ cup of vinegar.

When cleaning an asphalt tile floor with water, use a well-wrung cloth or sponge; excess water can seep into the seams and loosen the adhesives that hold the flooring.

Rather than wax floors on your hands and knees, stand and use a long-handled paint roller. A roller not only speeds up the waxing process, it makes it easy to reach under a radiator or built-in furniture.

To clean up raw egg dropped on a floor, sprinkle it with salt, let it sit for 15 to 20 minutes, and then sweep it up with a broom.

Instead of using a rag to apply paste wax to floors, get a better grip and protect your skin with a glove-type potholder or workman's glove slipped over your hand. Such gloves have the added advantage of being sturdy and easy to clean.

When washing highly waxed floors between wax-ings, use a solution of 1 cup of fabric softener in ½ pail of water to prevent dulling the shine.

A few drops of vinegar in the water used to clean the kitchen floor will help remove particles of cooking grease that have settled from the air.

For a fast shine between floor waxings, put a piece of waxed paper under your mop and slide it around your floor.

After you've waxed a floor, wrap a bath towel around each foot and shuffle around the room to polish the floor in a flash.

Carpets and Upholstery

Acid stains on a carpet or on upholstery should be immediately diluted and neutralized with baking soda and water, or with club soda. The same solutions will also keep vomit stains from setting.

If someone spills an alcoholic drink on carpet or upholstery, instantly dilute the spot with cold water so that the alcohol doesn't have time to attack the dyes. If red wine has been spilled, dilute it with white wine, then clean the spot with cold water and cover it with table salt. Wait 10 minutes, then vacuum up the salt.

Some homemakers use a paste of laundry starch and cold water to lift blood stains from carpet or upholstery. The paste is allowed to dry and then brushed away.

Dampen blood stains on carpet or upholstery with cold water. (Hot water *sets* the stains.) Then apply carpet or upholstery shampoo and follow this treatment by applying dry-cleaning fluid.

To remove chewing gum that is stuck on the carpet, press an ice cube against the gum. The gum will harden and can then be pulled off. Treat any last traces of gum with a spot remover.

Blot coffee stains quickly and dilute with plain water.

Use dry-cleaning fluid on tar spots, but apply it sparingly and blot regularly.

If there's candle wax on carpet or upholstery, put an ice cube in a plastic bag and hold it against the wax. When the wax becomes brittle, chip it away with a dull knife.

Here's another way to remove candle wax from carpet or upholstery: Place a blotter over the wax spot and press with a warm iron until the blotter absorbs the melted wax. Move the blotter frequently so that it doesn't get oversaturated.

You can occasionally remove crayon marks on carpet or upholstery by using the iron-and-blotter treatment that's effective with candle wax; you can also try dabbing at them using a cloth moistened with dry-cleaning fluid.

Absorb butter stains—and other greasy household stains on carpet or upholstery—with cornmeal, dried and ground corn cobs, or dry-cleaning fluid.

To remove nonbutter-type grease stains on carpet or upholstery, scrape up as much spilled grease as possible and apply dry-cleaning fluid with a cloth. Or rub with paint thinner, cover with salt, and vacuum. Another alternative: Sprinkle with cornmeal, leave overnight, and vacuum.

Use hair spray to lift ballpoint ink stains from carpet or upholstery. Use dry-cleaning fluid, applied with a cloth, on other ink stains. Here's another way to cope with ink stains: Sprinkle them with salt. As ink is absorbed, brush the salt away and sprinkle again. Repeat as necessary.

Try to remove mildew from carpet or upholstery with white vinegar. If spots remain, rub with dry-cleaning fluid. Note: Eliminate moist conditions or the mildew will return.

Lift nail polish with prepared polish removers or acetone, but apply these sparingly and with great care because they can damage the carpet or upholstery.

To remove wet latex paint spots on carpet or upholstery, dab with water. To remove wet oil-based paint spots, dab with turpentine, then absorb the turpentine with cornmeal. In either case, follow with an application of dry-cleaning fluid or shampoo.

Allow mud spots to dry, then brush softly to loosen the dirt and vacuum.

If your pets have accidents on carpet or upholstery, blot the stains with water, then clean with club soda. A mix of equal parts of white vinegar and water is also effective.

Remove animal hair from furniture by wiping with a damp sponge. Dabbing with pieces of Scotch tape also works well.

You can remove soot stains by sprinkling generously with salt, allowing the salt to settle for several minutes, and vacuuming both salt and soot.

The best way to clean vinyl upholstery is with baking soda on a damp cloth, followed by a light washing with a dishwashing soap. Never use oil; it will only harden the upholstery.

If your carpet sweeper misses lint, string, and other small debris, just dampen the brushes.

Carpet odors can be eliminated by sprinkling baking soda on the carpet before vacuuming, or by doing the same thing with 1 cup of borax mixed with 2 cups of cornmeal. (Let the latter mixture stand for an hour before vacuuming.)

Just as fabric softener takes static cling out of your laundry, it can remove static "shock" from your carpet. Spray your carpet lightly with a mix of 5 parts water and 1 part liquid softener and you won't have to worry about shocks when you touch metallic objects.

Rugs will last longer if you occasionally rotate them to change areas of wear, or if you rearrange furniture to alter traffic patterns.

To raise depressions left in carpets by heavy furniture, try steaming them. Hold an iron close enough for steam to reach the carpet, but don't let the iron touch the fibers, especially if they're synthetic, because they could melt. Lift the fibers by scraping them with the edge of a coin or spoon.

When a carpet thread is loose, snip it level with the pile. If you try to pull out the thread you risk unraveling part of the carpet.

To repair a large burned area in a carpet, cut out the damaged area and substitute a patch of identical size and shape. Secure the new piece with double-faced carpet tape and latex adhesive.

You needn't hide a carpet burn with furniture. If the burn isn't down to the backing, just snip off the charred part with fingernail scissors. However, if a carpet burn does extend to the backing, snip off the charred fibers and put white glue in the opening. Then, snip fibers from a scrap or an inconspicuous part of the carpet (perhaps in a closet). When the glue gets tacky, poke the fibers into place.

To prevent small area rugs from slipping out from under you, attach strips of double-faced carpet tape under the corners.

Walls and Wall Coverings

There's no need to purchase expensive wall cleaner. You can make your own economical cleaner by mixing into a gallon of warm water ¼ cup of washing soda, ¼ cup of white vinegar, and ½ cup of ammonia.

Lift crayon marks off a painted wall by rubbing them carefully with a cloth or sponge dampened with mineral spirits or lighter fluid. Remove any shine left on flat paint by sponging lightly with hot water.

To remove crayon marks on wallpaper, rub carefully with a dry soap-filled, fine grade steel-wool pad. Or use a wad of white paper toweling moistened with dry-cleaning solvent and delicately sponge the surface. Carefully blot and lift in small areas to prevent the solvent from spreading and discoloring the paper.

It's best to wash walls from the bottom up; otherwise, water trickling over the dry, unwashed areas creates hard-to-remove streaks.

You can make washing walls less of a wet, messy task by decreasing the amount of water and using an egg beater to make thick suds.

Remove ordinary soil marks from wallpaper by rubbing them gently with an art gum eraser.

It's easy to remove transparent tape from a wall without marring the paint or wallpaper if you press the tape—through a protective cloth—with a warm iron to soften and loosen the tape's adhesive backing.

For cleaning rough-textured walls, old nylon stockings or socks are better than sponges or cloths because they won't tear and leave difficult-to-remove bits and pieces on the surface.

You can sponge washable wall coverings and some vinyls with a mild detergent. To find out how much elbow grease your paper can take, first work on a scrap.

Lift grease stains from washable wallpaper with a paste made of cornstarch and water. Alternatively, rub dry borax over stains.

To remove grease stains from a grass-cloth wall or ceiling covering apply an aerosol dry cleaner. Follow instructions carefully.

To remove a grease spot from nonwashable wallpaper, place a blotter over the spot and press it with a moderately hot iron. The blotter will soak up the grease. Repeat as required.

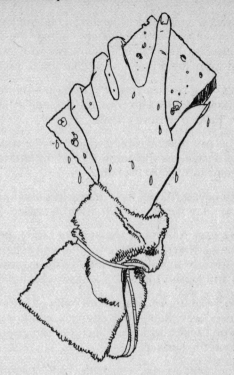

To prevent water from running down your arm when washing walls, fashion a bracelet from a sponge or washcloth held in place with a thick rubber band.

Clean nonwashable wallpaper with rye bread. Make a fist-sized wad of bread and rub it across discolorations and dirt.

You can also use talcum powder to remove a grease spot on nonwashable wallpaper. Dust on the talc with a powder puff, leave it for an hour and then brush it off. Repeat, if necessary.

To remove white water marks from wood wall paneling, rub mayonnaise into them. Wipe off the mayonnaise 12 hours later. The marks will have vanished.

Windows

A liquid cleaner for glass can be made by mixing 2 cups of water and 2 tablespoons of liquid dishwashing detergent with 2 cups of isopropyl rubbing alcohol (70 percent). Stir until thoroughly mixed and then pour into a clean, pump-spray bottle. The alcohol keeps the cleaner from freezing on the panes in cold weather.

Pure vinegar will remove stubborn hard-water sprinkler spots and streaks from a window.

Cloudy days are preferable to sunny days for window washing because direct sunlight dries cleaning solutions before you can polish the glass properly.

If you can wash one side of a window with horizontal strokes and the other side with vertical strokes, you'll be able to tell which side a streak is on.

An old auto wiper blade makes a good squeegee for washing windows.

When washing windows, a soft toothbrush or a cotton swab is a useful tool for cleaning corners.

It is possible to clean upstairs window exteriors without using a ladder. Use a garden hose spray bottle attachment containing automatic dishwasher detergent; the spray leaves only a few spots.

To give an extra shine to window glass, polish it with well-washed cotton T-shirts or old diapers.

Polish windows to a sparkling shine with crumpled-up newspaper. The paper also leaves a film that's resistant to dirt.

Rubbing a clean blackboard eraser over a freshly

washed (and dried) window gives it a diamond-bright shine.

To make an ammonia-based glass cleaner, mix 2 cups of water, 1 cup of isopropyl rubbing alcohol (70 percent), and 1 tablespoon of household ammonia. Pour into a clean, pump-spray bottle.

Window Treatments

To keep drapery hem folds in position, insert wire solder or plastic-covered wire. Bend the wire into the desired shapes after hanging the draperies.

Old keys make good drapery weights.

To prevent a curtain rod from snagging when sliding it through a curtain, slip a piece of aluminum foil or a thimble over its tip.

Do your draperies gap in the middle when you close them? They won't if you sew a small magnet into both center seams at the same height from the floor.

To make sure that curtain tie-backs are exactly opposite each other, use the bottom edge of the window shade as your guide when you install them.

Before washing a curtain, shake it outdoors to remove accumulated dust.

If you wear cotton gloves when washing Venetian blinds you can use your fingers to rub the slats—this works better than any brush. Another way to wash Venetian blinds is to hang them from a clothesline and turn a hose on them. You can also wash them under the shower. Use mild soap and water.

If you're interrupted while cleaning Venetian blinds, clasp a clothespin to the last slat you cleaned so you'll know where you left off.

To prevent Venetian blind tapes from shrinking when cleaned, rehang the blinds before the tapes dry.

Make yellowed Venetian blind tapes white again by applying liquid white shoe polish.

To install a new Venetian blind cord, tape or sew the end of the new one to the old one. Slowly pull out the old cord and you'll pull the new one into place at the same time.

Spray Venetian blind pulleys with a silicone lubricant to keep them working smoothly.

Use wallpaper cleaner or an art gum eraser to lift spots from window shades.

If an unwashable window shade needs cleaning, rub it with a rough flannel cloth dipped in cornmeal or flour.

A window shade that has too much tension can be removed from its bracket and unrolled by hand two or three revolutions to make it less tense after it is replaced.

A shade that won't lift properly needs more tension. Remove it, roll it up two or three revolutions, and reinstall it.

Use a silicone spray instead of oil on a window-shade mechanism. (Oil will soak through the wood roller and ruin your shade.)

The Bathroom

To make your own ceramic tile cleaner, put ¼ cup of baking soda, ½ cup of white vinegar, and 1 cup of household ammonia in a bucket. Add 1 gallon of warm water, stirring until the baking soda dissolves. Wearing rubber gloves, apply the mixture with a scrub brush or sponge and then rinse. Mix a fresh batch for each cleaning.

To make your own heavy-duty grout cleaner, put 3 cups of baking soda in a medium-size bowl and add 1 cup of warm water. Mix the contents to a smooth paste and scrub into grout with a damp sponge or toothbrush, rinsing thoroughly afterwards. Mix a fresh batch for each cleaning.

A typewriter eraser from the stationery store is an excellent tool for cleaning the grout between bathroom tiles.

To make your bathroom walls sparkle, rub the ceramic tile with car wax and buff after 10 minutes.

You can remove most mildew from the grout between tiles by rubbing it with a toothbrush or nailbrush dipped in laundry bleach. (Don't use abrasive powders or steel-wool pads or you'll scratch the tile. Rinse with clear water after cleaning. If spots remain, you could camouflage stained grout with a white fingernail pencil or white liquid shoe polish. (If you get polish on the tiles, let it dry and then wipe it off with a rag.)

One-quarter cup of sodium bisulfate (sodium acid sulfate) can be sprinkled into a wet toilet bowl for a single scrubbing and flushing. (Wear rubber gloves.) Let it stand for 15 minutes, and then scrub and flush as usual. (Don't use with chlorine bleach because the resulting fumes would be toxic.)

Rust stains under a toilet bowl rim sometimes yield to laundry bleach—but be sure to protect your hands with plastic or rubber gloves. (Note: Never combine bleach with toilet-bowl cleaners; the mix can release toxic gases.) Rub off truly stubborn stains with extra-fine steel wool, or with wet–dry sandpaper (available at hardware stores).

Cola that has gone flat can be spilled into the toilet bowl and left for an hour. The soft drink will clean the bowl.

Chemical toilet bowl cleaners should never be used to clean the bathtub or sink; the chemical will ruin the finish.

A ring around the tub can be rubbed away without cleaners with a nylon-net ball or pad. Cover a stubborn ring with a paste of cream of tartar and hydrogen peroxide. When the paste dries, wipe it off—along with the ring. To enjoy your bath without worrying about leaving a tub ring, add a capful of mild liquid dishwashing detergent to the bath water.

To get rid of rust stains on a bathtub, try rubbing them with a paste of borax powder and lemon juice. If the stain persists, use a dry-cleaning solution.

An old nylon stocking rolled into a ball becomes a nonscratch scrub pad for cleaning sink and tub.

Clean a rubber or vinyl bathtub mat by tossing it into the washer with bath towels. The terry cloth scrubs the mat, and everything comes out clean.

Shower enclosures are a chore to keep clean—but they can be less of a problem if you follow these suggestions: Keep mildew from taking hold by wiping shower walls with a towel after each shower, while you're still in the tub. When the walls need a thorough cleaning, run the shower water at its hottest temperature so the steam will loosen the dirt. Then, using a sponge mop, clean in a jiffy with a mixture of ½ cup vinegar, 1 cup clear ammonia, and ¼ cup baking soda in 1 gallon of warm water. After cleaning, rinse with clear water. Note: Never use harsh abrasive powders or steel-wool pads.

Having trouble getting mineral deposits off a

shower head? Remove the head, take it apart, and soak it in vinegar. Then brush deposits loose with an old toothbrush. Clean the holes by poking them with a wire, pin, toothpick, or ice pick.

Lemon oil will remove water spots on metal frames around shower doors and enclosures.

Glass shower doors will sparkle again if you clean them once a week with a sponge dipped in white vinegar.

To prevent shower curtains from wrinkling after washing, put them in the washing machine with ½ cup of detergent and ½ cup of baking soda, along with two large bath towels. Add a cup of vinegar to the rinse cycle, then hang the curtains up immediately after washing and let them air dry.

Keep a new shower curtain looking fresh by using the old shower curtain as a liner. Hang the new curtain on the same hooks, but in front of the old curtain. The old curtain will take the beating from water and soap scum while the new one stays squeaky clean.

When you clean a plastic shower curtain, keep it soft and flexible by adding a few drops of mineral oil to the rinse water. Maintain the curtain's softness by wiping it occasionally with a solution of warm water and mineral oil.

To make your bathroom mirror sparkle, polish it with a cloth dipped in a borax-and-water solution or in denatured alcohol. Or polish with dry facial tissue, a lint-free cloth, paper toweling, or old nylon stockings.

Rubbing alcohol will wipe away hair-spray haze on a mirror.

You can defog a bathroom mirror quickly by spraying it with hot air from a hair dryer.

General Home Maintenance

Flooring and Stairs

It you nave a squeaky wood floor under tile or carpet, you may be able to eliminate the squeak without removing the floor covering. Try to reset loose boards by pounding a hammer on a block of scrap wood in the area over the squeaky boards. The pressure may force loose nails back into place.

You may be able to silence squeaky hardwood floors by using talcum powder as a dry lubricant. Sprinkle powder over the offending areas, and sweep it back and forth until it filters down between the cracks.

Try filling dents in a hardwood floor with clear nail polish or shellac. Because the floor's color will show through, the dents will not be apparent.

Sometimes you can flatten bulges or curled seams in a linoleum floor by placing aluminum foil over them and "ironing" them with your steam iron. (The heat will soften and reactivate the adhesive.) Position weights, such as stacks of books, over treated areas to keep them flat until the adhesive cools and hardens.

To remove a resilient floor tile for replacement, lay a piece of aluminum foil on it and then press down with an ordinary iron set at medium. The iron's heat will soften the mastic, and you can easily pry up the tile with a putty knife.

To remove a damaged resilient tile, soften it with a propane torch fitted with a flame-spreader nozzle. (Be careful not to damage surrounding tiles.) When the tile is soft, pry it up with a paint scraper or putty knife and scrape the adhesive off the floor so that the new tile bonds cleanly.

To patch a gouge (not a dent) in a resilient floor, take a scrap of the flooring and grate it with a food grater. Mix the resulting dust with clear nail polish and plug the hole.

Another way to camouflage a gouge or hole in a resilient floor is with crayon wax. Choose a crayon that matches the floor color, melt it, fill the gouge or hole, and then wax the floor.

To prevent scratching the floor when moving heavy furniture across uncarpeted areas, slip scraps of old carpeting, face down, under all furniture legs.

After laying floor tiles, you can help them lie flat by going over them with a rolling pin.

Solvent-based cleaners and polishes preserve cork tile floors and should be used instead of water or water-based products.

So chairs won't scratch a hardwood floor, glue bunion pads to the bottoms of the chair legs.

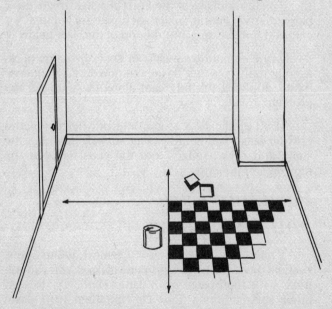

Install floor tiles from the center of a room outward, because the center of a room is where appearance and perfect matching are most important.

To make a bathroom carpet fit perfectly, make a precise pattern with paper. Lay overlapped sheets of paper on the bathroom floor, tightly butted up against corners, walls, and obstacles. Tape the sheets together and cut. Turn the pattern over, face down, on the back of the carpet, trace with a pencil, and then cut.

If you want to replace a damaged area of resilient flooring, here's a way to make a perfect patch from scrap flooring: Place the scrap piece over the damaged area so that it overlaps sufficiently, and tape it to hold it in place. Then, cut through both layers at the same time to make a patch that is an exact duplicate. Replace the damaged area with the tightly fitting patch.

To stop squeaks at the front of a stair tread, drive pairs of spiral flooring nails, each pair angled in a "V," across the tread and into the top of the riser below it.

Try eliminating squeaks in stairs by using packaged graphite powder or talcum powder in a squeeze bottle, applying the lubricant along the joints in the problem area.

If an application of graphite powder or talcum powder fails to eliminate a stair squeak, go under the stairs and drive wedges into the gaps between the moving components.

Furniture Care and Refinishing

There are several ways to remove white spots, such as those left by wet drinking glasses. You can rub them with toothpaste on a damp cloth. (Try this on other surface stains, too.) Or rub them with paste furniture polish, any mild abrasive, or oil. Appropriate abrasives are ashes, salt, soda, or pumice; suitable oils are olive oil, petroleum jelly, cooking oil, or lemon-oil furniture polish.

You can tighten a loose furniture leg caster by wrapping a rubber band around its stem and reinserting it.

When wood fibers in a piece of furniture are merely bent, but not cut, straighten out any dents with an iron, set on medium, and a damp cloth. Place the damp cloth on a dent, hold the iron on it until the cloth begins to dry, redampen the cloth, and repeat the process as needed.

Tighten a cabinet or dresser knob by dipping its screw or screws in fingernail polish or shellac and reinserting the knob. When the polish or shellac hardens, the screws will be set and the knobs will be tight.

It's best to position a piano where the sun won't shine on it and where it's least likely to be exposed to changes in temperature or humidity.

You can unstick wooden drawers by rubbing contact surfaces with a bar of soap or a candle.

A coat of wax prevents rusting on chrome kitchen chairs.

Paper stuck to a polished table can be lifted after saturating the paper with cooking oil.

Decals will easily lift off painted furniture if you sponge with vinegar.

To tighten wobbly wicker furniture, wash it outdoors with hot soapy water, rinse it with a hose, and let it air dry. The wood and cane will shrink and tighten.

Saggy wicker or cane seats can be similarly tightened by sponging them with hot water.

Sometimes a warped table leaf or other board can be straightened by exposure to wet grass and hot summer sun. For this treatment, water a grassy area thoroughly and set the board, concave side down, on the wet grass. As the dry side of the board absorbs moisture from the grass, the moist (convex) side is dried out by the sun and the board unwarps. This process takes no longer than a day.

If you need to pound apart sections of a chair that needs regluing, a soft mallet will provide enough power but will be much kinder to the wood than a hammer.

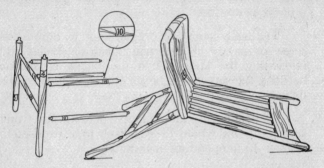

When disassembling a piece of furniture for repair, label or number the parts with pieces of masking tape so you'll know how to put them together again. Make a list describing which part of the piece of furniture each number represents. For example, number 10—top right-side rung (as you're facing the chair).

Thread can serve as packing around a chair rung before it is reglued.

When using paint stripper on a piece of furniture that has legs, put a tin can under each leg to catch drips. This protects the floor and lets you reuse the stripper that collects in the cans.

Use a tourniquet to hold a freshly glued chair rung firmly in place. Clamp the glued rung with a heavy cord wrapped around the chair legs. Use a dowel to twist the cord until the proper tension is reached, then prop the dowel to maintain pressure.

If a chair wobbles because one leg is shorter than the others, steady the chair by forming an appropriately shaped piece of wood putty to "extend" the short leg. When the putty dries, sand and stain it to match the leg and glue it in place.

When gluing dowels, a dowel that's exactly the size of the hole it fits into can push much of the glue to the bottom of the hole and therefore not hold as well as it should. To avoid this, cut a few grooves in the dowel so the glue is distributed along its surface for a more secure bond.

It's a practical idea to use newspaper to protect your floor or workbench when you're refinishing a piece of furniture, but the legs may stick to the paper. To avoid this, drive a nail part of the way into the bottom of each leg.

When you're working with varnish, hold the container as still as possible so that bubbles don't form and spoil the smooth finish.

If you'd like to know how your unfinished furniture would look if it were stained, try the "wet test." Dampen a cloth with turpentine and wipe it over the surface; the moisture will bring out the grain, showing any contrasts and giving the wood the appearance it would have if stained.

Sanding concave curves will be easier if you hold the sandpaper around a piece of dowel the same diameter as the curve or smaller. Or, slit a length of rubber garden hose and wrap the paper around it, with the ends held in the slit.

To sand a furniture spindle or rung without flattening it, hold a sandpaper strip behind the part, one end in each hand, and saw the ends back and forth to buff-sand the wood.

For scraping small areas when refinishing, consider using such unconventional tools as a coin, bottle cap, golf tee, screwdriver, or your thumbnail. Even a car windshield scraper can be pressed into service.

When refinishing, a flat rubber kitchen spatula can be a useful scraper for removing paint from curved or rounded surfaces, especially since it can be used even on delicate carvings. For greater versatility, buy both wide and narrow sizes.

Many small items are useful for cleaning furniture crevices and cracks when you're refinishing. Enlist the aid of a nut pick, a plastic playing card, a plastic credit card, the broken end of an ice cream stick, the tine of an old fork, an orange stick, wood toothpicks, or an old spoon.

If you need an unusually shaped smoothing tool for use on wet spackling compound and other wood fillers, try whittling an ice cream stick to the required contour.

A heavy string is useful when stripping the narrow turnings of a spindle furniture leg. Gently "saw" the string back and forth to remove the finish.

To avoid gouging wood when using a putty knife to strip furniture, round the putty knife's sharp corners with a fine-toothed file. If you're working on large flat surfaces, dull a paint scraper the same way.

Remember that treatment with any bleach raises the wood grain, even when the furniture piece has been thoroughly sanded. To prevent the raised grain from affecting the finish, resand to the level of the wood surface after the wood dries.

To obtain a smooth, evenly finished surface on open-grained woods, treat them with a filler after staining. First apply filler in the direction of the grain; then work across the grain to fill all pores completely.

If large knots in unfinished furniture are loose, remove them, apply carpenters' glue around their edges, and replace them flush with the surface. If small knots (pin knots) are loose, remove and discard them and plug the resulting holes with plastic wood or water putty.

For the most professional patching job, use shellac sticks to fill cracks and gouges since they leave the least conspicuous patch.

It will be easier to apply paint or varnish remover to a piece of furniture if all hardware has been removed. If you label the hardware along with a sketch of the furniture, it will also be easier to reassemble it correctly.

If hardware is spotted with paint or finish, drop it into a pan filled with paint remover. Let it soak while you work on the wood, then wipe it clean.

Small blisters on a veneered surface can sometimes be flattened with heat. Here's how: Lay a sheet of smooth cardboard over the blistered area and press firmly with a medium-hot iron, moving the iron slowly and evenly until the blisters soften and flatten. Leave the cardboard in place and weight the smoothed-out area for 24 hours.

To help slow evaporation after applying a coat of paint remover—and give it more time to work—cover the surface with aluminum foil. Keep in mind, though, that paint remover stops working in any case after about 40 minutes.

You can make a template to patch damaged veneer this way: Lay a sheet of bond paper over the damaged area and rub a soft lead pencil gently over the paper. The edges of the damaged area will be precisely indicated on the paper so you can cut a pattern.

For more durability, top an antiqued finish with a coat of semi-gloss or high-gloss varnish.

If you apply a protective shellac coating to cane chair seats they'll last longer and be easier to clean.

When you reupholster furniture, put fabric scraps in an envelope and staple the envelope to the underside of the newly covered piece. That way you'll have the scraps you may later need for patching.

When using ornamental tacks for upholstery, push extras into the frame in an inconspicuous spot so you have replacements if needed.

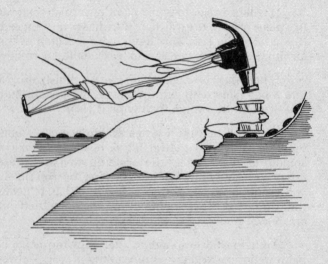

To hammer decorative furniture tacks without damaging their heads, place a wooden spool over each tack and pound on the spool.

Before covering kitchen chair seats with plastic, warm the plastic with a heating pad so it will be more pliable and easier to handle.

For speed and convenience, you can cut foam rubber upholstery padding with an electric carving knife.

Maintaining and Repairing Windows

Spattered rain and dirt will easily wipe off window sills that have a protective coat of wax.

Applying a reflective vinyl coating on the inside of your windows will both protect your furniture upholstery or drapery fabric from the fading effects of strong sunlight and help keep your home cooler in the summertime.

To free a window that's been painted shut, use a scraper, knife, or spatula to cut the paint seal between the sash and the window frame. Then, working from the outside, insert the blade of a pry bar under the sash and pry gently from the corners in. Lever the bar over a block of scrap wood.

When replacing a broken sash cord, consider using a sash chain, which lasts much longer.

Soften old putty for easy removal by heating it with a soldering iron, propane torch, or handheld hair dryer. Or, if you prefer, soften it with linseed oil and then scrape it away.

To prevent a window pane crack from spreading, score a small arc with a glass cutter just beyond the crack, curving around it. Usually the crack will travel only as far as the arc.

To remove cracked glass from a window without excessive splintering, crisscross the pane on both sides with several strips of masking tape, then rap it with a hammer. Most of the pane will be held together.

If you try to open a window and it refuses to budge, tap a hammer on a block of wood at various places on the sash. (Don't hit the sash directly with the hammer, or you'll leave dents.) The tapping may jar the sash loose.

To make dried-out putty workable again, sprinkle it with a few drops of raw linseed oil and knead it until it is soft and pliable.

Before attempting to chisel dried and hardened putty from a wooden window frame, brush raw linseed oil over the putty's surface. Let it soak in to soften the putty.

You can fill a pellet gun hole in a window pane with clear nail polish or shellac. Dab at the hole; when the application dries, dab again—and reapply until the hole is filled. The pane will appear clear. A pellet-gun hole in stained glass can be filled the same way.

When installing a new window pane, speed up the process by rolling the glazing compound between the palms of your hands to form a long string the diameter of a pencil. Lay the "string" along the frame, over the glass, and smooth it in place with a putty knife.

When glazing windows, brush the frames where the putty will lie with boiled linseed oil to prevent the wood from drinking the oils from the putty.

If you want to cover your clear bathroom window without putting up curtains, render the glass opaque by brushing on a mixture of 4 tablespoons of Epsom salts and ½ pint of stale beer. Alternatives: Glue on stained-glass pieces, silver Mylar, or wax paper. Double-duty alternative: Cover the panes with mirrored squares, which, as a side benefit, will make the bathroom seem larger.

If the putty knife sticks or pulls at the glazing compound when you're glazing a window, "grease" the knife by dipping the blade into linseed oil. Wipe off the excess.

When painting glazing compound, lap the paint slightly over the edge of the compound and onto the glass.

Maintaining and Repairing Screens

To keep aluminum screens from pitting, clean them outdoors (never indoors) with kerosene. Dip a rag in the kerosene and rub both sides of the mesh and the frames, then wipe off the excess. This is a particularly good rust-inhibitor for older screens. (Since kerosene is highly flammable, it should always be stored in small amounts in a cool place.)

To repair a small tear in a wire window screen, push the wire strands back into place with an ice pick. If the hole doesn't close completely, brush clear nail polish or shellac sparingly across the remaining opening. Let the sealer dry, and reapply until the pinhole is transparently sealed. (Be careful not to let any sealer run down the screen; immediately blot any excess.)

Clean awnings in the direction of the seam, not against it. As fabric awnings age, their seams weaken.

You can rejuvenate faded canvas awnings with a special paint available from awning dealers or paint stores.

If there's a clean cut or tear in a window screen, you can stitch it together. Use a long needle and a strong nylon thread or a fine wire. Zigzag stitch across the cut, being careful not to pull the thread or wire so tight that the patch puckers. After stretching, apply clear nail polish to keep the thread or wire from pulling loose.

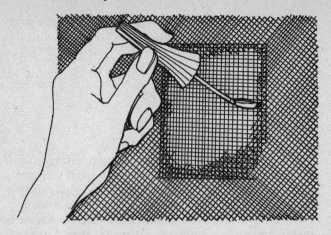

To close a large hole in a window screen, cut a patch from a scrap piece of screening of the same type as the damaged screen. Zigzag stitch the patch into place, and then apply clear nail polish to the stitching.

To repair fiberglass screening, lay a fiberglass patch over the hole or tear with a piece of foil over it, and run a hot iron around the edges; the heat fuses the patch to the screen. The foil prevents the iron from touching the screen directly.

Lower rolled-up awnings after a storm to allow them to dry.

Maintaining and Repairing Doors

If hinge screws on a door are loose because the screw holes have become enlarged, fill the holes with pieces of wood toothpick dipped in glue. When the glue dries, reinsert the screws. Or, wrap hinge screws with steel wool and reinsert.

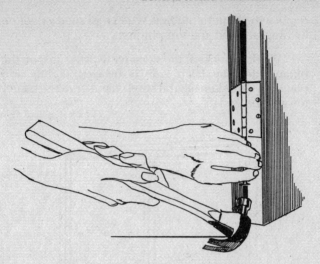

If you're trying to remove a door's hinge pin and the pin won't budge, press a nail against the hinge bottom and tap upward against the nail with a hammer.

If a door binds on the knob side when the door is closed, its hinges may be misaligned. If the top of the knob side binds, try putting a cardboard shim behind the bottom hinge. If the bottom corner binds, slip a cardboard shim behind the top hinge. To shim a door hinge, loosen the screws on the door frame side. Cut a shim from thin cardboard with slots to fit around the screws, slide it behind the hinge, and tighten the screws.

Children old enough to answer the door should be able to see who's there, just as you do. Install a second peephole low enough for youngsters to use.

If a doorknob bangs against a wall, protect the wall by covering the knob with a slit-open powder puff.

For better control when lifting a door off its hinges,

remove the bottom pin first. When replacing a door on its hinges, insert the top pin first.

If a door sticks at the sides, try to plane only on the hinge side. The latch side is beveled slightly and planing could damage the bevel. Plane from the center toward the ends.

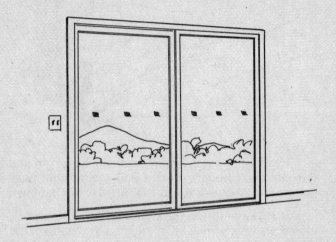

To prevent people from mistaking a closed sliding glass door for an open one, apply eye-level decals—at both adult and child levels if necessary—to alert people before they walk into the pane and possibly injure themselves. You can use the same trick to mark lightweight screens.

You needn't worry about oil dripping on the floor if you quiet a squeaky hinge by lubricating its pin with petroleum jelly rather than oil.

Cardboard shields will protect the finish on a door when you clean and polish door hardware. Fit the shields around the pertinent metal parts, holding them in place with masking tape.

If you have to remove some wood at a door's binding points, use a block plane on the top or bottom of the door and a jack plane to work on the side. Work from the ends to the center on the top or bottom edge, from the center out on the sides.

When you've fashioned a door to the exact size for hanging, bevel the latch edge backward just a bit to let it clear the jamb as it swings open and shut.

If you need to plane the bottom of a door because it scrapes the threshold or the floor, you can do so without removing the door. Place sandpaper on the threshold or floor, then move the door back and forth over this abrasive surface. Slide a newspaper or magazine under the sandpaper if it needs to be raised in order to make contact.

Before you replace a door that you have planed, seal the planed edges. If you don't, the raw wood will absorb moisture and the door will swell and stick again.

Graphite from a soft pencil can be used to lubricate a resistant door lock. Rub the key across the pencil point, and then slide it in and out of the lock several times.

If you want to replace an existing lock but you can't find a new one that will fit the existing holes, cover the old holes with a large decorative escutcheon plate.

Home Lighting and Electricity

Safety is an important consideration when you're working with electricity. To make sure that no one accidentally flips the circuit breaker back on while you're making electrical repairs, put a piece of tape— and a sign to let people know what you're doing—over the handle of the circuit breaker. The same precaution applies to a fuse box.

Wait to tinker with a switch outlet or lighting fixture—even though you've flicked off the switch—until you have also deactivated the circuit. In many switching systems, parts of the circuit are still energized when the switch is off.

When working with electricity, insulate your pliers by slipping a length of small-diameter rubber hose on each handle. Wrap other metal parts with electrician's tape. Insulate the shank of a screwdriver by slipping a section of rubber or plastic tubing over it. Be sure to cut the tubing so that it extends from the handle down to the blade.

Replace a fuse with one of the same amperage as the one you took out. You risk causing an electrical fire if you use a fuse rated to carry more amps or if you try to bypass the fuse in any way.

Save time ahead of time. Determine which circuits activate which outlets in your home; then diagram or print the information on a card attached to your circuit breaker or fuse box. When your electricity fails, you'll be able to solve the problem quickly.

For safety's sake, stand on a dry board when working with a fuse box or a circuit-breaker box. Also use a wooden rather than an aluminum stepladder to minimize the risk or shock when working with electrical wiring.

Everyone in the family should know how to throw the master switch that cuts off all electrical current. Any time there's a chance of contact between water and electricity, avoid wading in water until the master switch has been shut off.

When maneuvering a section of electrical cable through a wall, play it safe and use roughly 20 percent

more than a straight-line measurement indicates that
you need. Often there are unexpected obstructions and
the cable must be moved around. You can cut off any
extra cable.

A blown fuse or a tripped circuit breaker is a sign
of trouble. Locate and eliminate the problem before you
replace a blown fuse or reset a tripped circuit breaker.
Otherwise the problem will only recur.

So that you won't be left in the dark if a bulb burns
out in the basement, light the area with a two-socket
fixture. If one bulb burns out, the other will still enable
you to see.

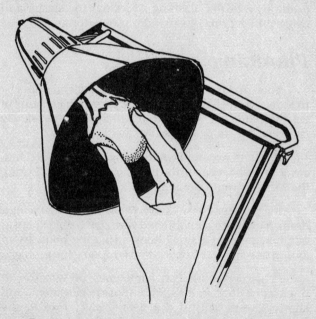

If it's difficult to remove a broken light bulb
because there's little left to grasp, turn off the switch,
jam a sponge-rubber ball against the jagged glass, and
twist.

If you're distracted by shadows that reduce visibility in your kitchen or workshop, replace incandescent fixtures with fluorescent lamps which provide even, shadow-free illumination.

If you're planning to replace a lamp socket, consider installing a three-way socket for greater lighting versatility. Wiring a three-way socket is as simple as wiring a standard on/off fixture.

Any change in a fluorescent lamp's normal performance, such as flickering or noticeable dimming, is a warning that the bulb should be replaced. Failure to replace the bulb can strain parts of the fixture; for example, repeated flashing wears out the starter and causes the starter's insulation to deteriorate.

Plumbing

You can keep drains free of clogging and odors by this once-a-week treatment: Pour three tablespoons of washing soda (sal soda) into the drain and then slowly run very hot water to dissolve any build-ups.

For better suction when plunging a clogged drain, cover the rubber cap of the plunger with water and plug the fixture's vent opening with wet rags.

If a plunger doesn't work when you try to unclog a drain, try using a straightened wire coat hanger, bent at one end to form a small hook. Using the hook, try to loosen or remove the debris that is causing the problem.

A garden hose can sometimes be effective in unclogging floor drains such as those in basements and showers, especially if the debris isn't close to the opening. Attach the hose to a faucet, feed the hose into the drain as far as it will go, and jam rags around the hose at the opening. Then turn on the water full force for a few moments to blast the debris away.

If you hear a squealing noise when you turn the handle of a faucet, the metal threads of the stem are binding against the threads of the faucet. To fix this, remove the handle and stem and coat both sets of threads with petroleum jelly. The lubrication should stop the noise and make the handle easier to turn.

For a homemade, noncorrosive drain cleaner, mix 1 cup of baking soda, 1 cup of table salt, and ¼ cup of cream of tartar in a small bowl. Stir thoroughly and pour into a clean, covered jar. To use, pour ¼ cup of the mixture into the drain and immediately add 1 cup of boiling water. Wait 10 seconds, then flush with cold water. Do this weekly to keep drains clog-free and odorless. (One blending of this mixture equals 2¼ cups of cleaner.)

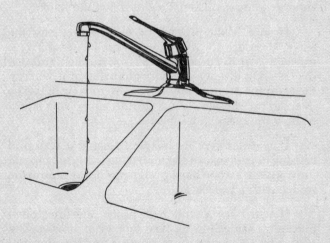

If a dripping faucet is getting on your nerves before the plumber arrives or before you have time to fix it yourself, tie a 2-foot-long string around the nozzle, and drop the string's end into the drain. As the faucet drips, the drops will run silently down the string and away.

What can you do if too little water comes from the tank to flush the toilet bowl clean? Check the water level in the tank, and if it doesn't come to within 1½ inches of the top of the overflow tube, bend the float arm up slightly to allow more water to enter the tank.

If there's very little water in a clogged toilet bowl, flushing will only cause the bowl to overflow. Instead, use a plunger to unclog the toilet; bring water from another source to cover the plunger cup for better suction.

To make a septic tank activator, combine in a large bowl 2 envelopes of active dry yeast with 1 pound of brown sugar; add 4 cups of warm water, stirring until the mixture completely blends. Set the mixture in a warm place for 10 to 20 minutes until it's foamy and its volume increases. Then, flush it down the toilet.

If your water pipes bang and faucets leak, the water pressure in your home may be reaching or exceeding 70 to 80 pounds per square inch and you may need to install a pressure-reducing valve. You can measure the average water pressure in your house by attaching a pressure gauge to the cold-water faucet nearest the main shut-off valve.

If a water pipe is banging against a wall and causing noise, you can silence it by wedging the pipe off the wall with a wood block and clamping the pipe to the wedge with a pipe strap.

If you have a stretch of water pipe that often freezes, consider buying heat tape (sometimes called heat cable). The tape is wrapped around the pipe and an automatic thermostat starts the heat when the outside temperature drops to about 35°F.

When thawing a frozen pipe, start at the tap end and open the tap so that melting ice and steam can run off or dissipate harmlessly. If you start at the middle of a pipe, steam from melting ice may burst the pipe.

When you're using hot water faucets regularly, there's no danger of hydrogen gas building up in your water heater. But if you've been away for an extended period, this danger does exist. If you've been away for awhile, open all hot water taps for a few minutes to prevent the danger of an explosion.

Good sweat solderers gain their expertise through practice. Buy a few short lengths of copper pipe and some fittings and practice before you tackle the real project.

To clean copper pipe before sweat soldering, wrap a strip of emery cloth around the end of the pipe and move it back and forth as if you were buffing a shoe.

Most amateur plumbers are so proud of their first sweat-soldered joints that they immediately turn on the water—a big mistake. Allow the joint to cool naturally, because the sudden cooling effect of rushing water can weaken the joint and cause it to crack.

If a pipe springs a leak, consider replacing an entire section rather than just patching the leak. A pipe that is sufficiently corroded to leak in one place will often start leaking in other places as well.

Whenever you secure a pipe, be careful to anchor it so that it can expand and contract with temperature changes. If you place a bracket on a pipe, include a buffer fashioned from garden hose, radiator hose, foam rubber, rubber cut from old inner tubes, or kitchen sponges.

To avoid having the teeth of the wrench scar a chrome-plated plumbing fixture during installation, first wrap the fixture with a double coating of plastic electrical tape.

To keep the water shut-off valve in good working order, turn it off and then on again once every 6 months.

Make sure everyone in the family knows where in your home the main shut-off valve is located. Also make sure everyone knows how to use it. This could prevent flooding in an emergency.

Soundproofing

Heavy, lined curtains will absorb excess noise in a room. Placing heavy furniture against the wall facing noisy neighbors will also help cut down on sounds.

To reduce noise in your home and cut energy costs at the same time, weatherstrip all doors and windows.

To insulate your home from street noise, double glaze the windows, insulate the walls and ceilings, and install wall-to-wall carpeting.

Cover hardwood floors with area rugs to cut down on noise in your home. Upholstered furniture also absorbs noise, while glass, chrome, and wood reflect noise.

Pest Control

You can keep ants away from your home with a concoction of borax and flour. Mix 1 cup of flour and 2 cups of borax in a quart jar. Punch holes in the jar's lid and sprinkle its contents outdoors around the foundation of your home.

Bothered by ants and other tiny insects in your cupboards? Scrub the cupboards and then leave several bay leaves in each to discourage return visits.

Bat-proofing your property is a good idea if you've been infested once and want to eliminate future colonies. The strong odor a colony leaves behind attracts other bats even after the first group has been evicted.

If you see a bat in your house, try to knock it to the floor with a tennis racquet or broom. Once it's stunned, pick it up wearing gloves, or scoop it up with a piece of paper, and get rid of it. Never handle a bat with your bare hands because of the risk of rabies.

If bees are nesting in a wall but you don't know exactly where, tap the wall at night and decide where the buzzing is loudest. Because the temperature inside the nest is usually about 95°F, you may also be able to feel its heat through the wall. Double check by drilling a small hole in the suspect area. If the drill bit comes out with honey or paraffin on it, you've found the nest.

Some people are allergic to bee or wasp stings. If you know or suspect that you are one of them, never try to exterminate a nest yourself. Have someone else do it.

If there's a hornet, wasp, bee, or other flying insect in your house and you have no insect spray, kill it with hair spray.

If your home becomes infested with fleas, vacuum rugs thoroughly before spraying and throw out the dust bag at once.

Mealworms, which are attracted to open packages of spaghetti, noodles, or macaroni, are repelled by spearmint chewing gum. You won't be bothered by the pests if you place a few sticks of wrapped gum in or near the packages. (Note: The gum must be wrapped so that it won't dry out and lose its scent.)

The scent of peppermint repels mice. To discourage these rodents, place sprigs of this herb where the rodents are likely to enter the house. You can achieve the same effect by soaking pieces of cardboard in oil of peppermint and leaving them in appropriate places.

Raw bacon or peanut butter makes good bait for a mousetrap; so does a cotton ball saturated with bacon grease. So that a mouse can't get the bait without springing the trap, make sure it will have to tug to remove the bait. If you're using peanut butter, dab some on the triggering device and let it harden before setting the trap. If bacon is your bait, tie it around the triggering device.

If you live in a multi-unit building, any pest control measures you take individually will be ineffective in the long run simply because insects can travel from one apartment to another. To eliminate bugs completely, the entire building should be treated at one time.

Since mosquito larvae thrive in water, changing the water in the birdbath every three days will help reduce the mosquito population.

Because raccoons carry fleas, take immediate action if one sets up housekeeping in your attic or chimney. Chemical repellents such as oil of mustard are temporarily effective, but the smell may bother you as much as it does the raccoon. Your best bet is to let the animal leave, and then cover its entrance hole with wire mesh so that it cannot return.

In the spring, moving leftover firewood away from the house will help discourage insect infestations.

Centipedes prey on other bugs, so the presence of centipedes in your house may indicate the presence of other insects as well.

The presence of carpenter ants indicates another problem. Because they're fond of damp wood, you should check your pipes, roof, and window sills for water leaks.

You can distinguish termite damage from other insect damage by examining any holes you find in wood. Termites eat only the soft part of wood, leaving the annual rings intact.

You can control roaches with a mixture of ½ cup of borax and ¼ cup of flour. Sprinkle this powder along baseboards and door sills, or spoon it into clear jar caps positioned under sinks or under cabinets.

Remember that supermarkets and grocery stores almost always have roaches, so check bags and boxes when unpacking food at home.

To keep rodents out of your house, seal every opening they could squeeze through. Some need less than a ¼-inch space. Put poison in deep cracks or holes, and stuff these with steel wool or scouring pads pushed in with a screwdriver. Close the spaces with spackling compound mixed with steel wool fragments.

Painting and Decorating

General Painting Tips

Prevent drips when painting a drawer front by removing the drawer and painting it face up.

Keep paint off window panes by masking pane edges with tape. If you have no tape, use strips of newspaper dampened so that they will stick to the glass. Peel off the paper as you finish each frame.

To avoid smearing when painting cabinets, paint the inside of the cabinets first. Then paint the tops, bottoms, and sides of doors before painting the door fronts. If you proceed in this sequence, you won't have to reach over already painted areas.

Protect doorknobs when painting doors by wrapping the knobs with aluminum foil or by slipping plastic sandwich bags over them.

Glue paper plates to paint can bottoms to serve as drip catchers. The plates move along with the cans and are more convenient than newspapers.

When painting stairs, paint alternate steps so that you'll have a way out. When those dry, paint the others. Or, paint one side of each step at a time. Use the other side for foot traffic until the painted side dries, then reverse the process.

Where appearance isn't important, steps will be safer if you mix in a little sand when painting them (so that they'll be less slippery) and edge them with luminous paint (so that they'll be more visible).

If your wall-switch cover plate was painted over along with the wall and you now need to remove it, avoid flaking or chipping any paint by cutting carefully around the plate's edge with a single-edge razor blade. Remove the screws and lift off the plate.

You'll be able to reach to paint the ceiling if you stand on a scaffold made by laying a wide plank across two sturdy chairs.

Before painting a ceiling, turn off the light fixture, loosen it, and let it hang down. Then wrap it in a plastic bag for protection against paint splatters.

If you don't want to—or can't—remove hardware when painting adjacent areas, coat the hardware with petroleum jelly before painting. You'll be able to wipe off any paint that gets on the metal by accident.

If the smell of fresh paint bothers you, you can eliminate it from a room in one day by leaving either a dish of ammonia or vinegar in the room, or onion slices in a bowl of water.

To cut the smell when you're decorating with oil-based paint, stir a spoonful of vanilla extract into each can of paint.

Don't wipe your paintbrush against the lip of the paint can. The lip will soon fill up with paint which will run down the side and drip off. Use a coffee can to hold the paint instead.

Wrinkling occurs when too much paint is applied or when the paint is too thick. You can correct wrinkling easily by sanding the surface and brushing on paint of a lighter consistency.

If you want to be able to use a previous coat of exterior paint as a base for a new coat, the old paint should be no more than five years old. If you wait longer than that you'll have a major job of scraping, sanding, and spackling.

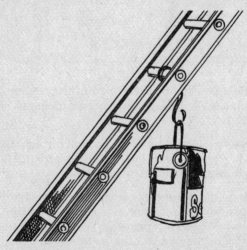

Make a paint holder from a coat hanger to keep your hands free when painting. Open the hanger and bend it in half; then bend it into an "S" to hook over the ladder and hold your paint can.

Artificial light darkens color, so your paint will look lighter in the daylight. If in doubt when at the paint store, take the container outside to examine the color.

All paint dries to a lighter shade than the one you see when it's first applied to the surface you're painting.

Color can saturate your eyes. When mixing paint, look away at a white surface for several minutes to allow your eyes to adjust so that you can judge the color accurately.

To get the correct "feel" for spray painting and to determine the correct spray distance from the object to be painted, first experiment with a sheet of cardboard as the target area.

To avoid painting a window shut, gently slide the sash up and down as the paint hardens but before it forms a seal.

If you are working on a ladder in front of a closed door, lock the door so that no one can inadvertently swing the door open and send you sprawling.

Record how much paint is required to cover each room by writing the amount on the back of a light-switch plate. When you remove the switch plate before repainting, you'll be reminded of how much fresh paint you need.

Do tiny spots need a paint touch-up? If you use cotton swabs instead of a brush, you won't waste paint and you won't have to clean a brush.

Outdoor Painting

When positioning a ladder against a house or tree, it is safest to position it so that the distance from the base of the ladder to the house or tree is one quarter of the ladder's extended length. Otherwise the ladder may fall forward or tip backward.

Spring is the ideal time to paint the exterior of a house. Do it as soon as the weather turns warm enough, but before the temperature gets too hot. In very hot weather paint dries too quickly and leaves marks where strokes were overlapped.

When painting the outside of your house, fold newspapers over the tops of doors and then close them. You won't paint the doors shut.

Don't use a flame to soften alligatored paint. The flame can shoot into a crack and ignite the sheathing.

Paint will not bond on a surface wet from morning dew or on a prime coat not thoroughly dry. And without proper bonding, paint will peel. Be sure to wait for dew to dry before painting.

If using an oil-based paint on an area that has suffered mildew, add a mildew inhibitor to the paint. (This isn't necessary with water-based paints, which don't contain the oil that fungus feeds on.)

Painting gutters is easy, but downspouts can be tricky. To protect the interior of the downspout against rust, drop a string with a weight on it down through the spout, and tie a sponge to the bottom end of the string. Use a sponge that must be compressed to fit inside the spout. Using plenty of paint, soak the sponge, and then pull on the string to squeeze the sponge up through the spout. The paint will spread evenly from bottom to top as the sponge goes up.

To prepare old wood for paint it's not necessary to remove the old paint. Simply seal all knots with thinned shellac and sand when dry. If the knot is loose, tighten it with wood caulking.

If you must leave a paint brush for a short time and don't want to clean it, wrap it in foil or a plastic bag to keep it soft and pliable. Put it in the freezer to save it for a longer time.

To avoid marring a paint job when leaning a ladder against clapboard siding, cover the top ends of the ladder with heavy woolen socks. The paint will remain unmarked.

If paint is blistering on hollow porch posts or columns, trapped moisture could be the problem. Cure it by boring small ventilating holes at the top and bottom of each post or column.

Don't use a sander with a revolving disc to remove paint from wood siding. It will gouge the surface.

Use a wire brush to remove loose and peeling paint from curved metal surfaces. A scraper or putty knife will take such paint off flat surfaces. Use steel wool on rust spots, and a mirror to inspect the undersides that you can't see otherwise.

Plant or prune shrubbery or trees so branches don't touch painted exterior surfaces. The undersides of leaves hold moisture long after a rain, and prolonged moisture causes paint to blister and peel.

When painting the exterior of your house, protect nearby shrubs from paint splatters by covering them with drop cloths or old sheets.

Raw metal is coated with a protective, oily film that keeps paint from adhering properly, so it's best to paint galvanized metal after it has weathered for at least six months. If you prefer not to wait for the metal to weather, strip the film by washing the metal with pure white vinegar. Rinse the metal with water and allow to dry before painting.

Cleanup and Storage

Before capping leftover paint for storage, mark the label at the level of the remaining paint so you'll know at a glance—without opening the can—how much is left inside. Label the cans by rooms so there's no question which paint to reorder or use for touch-ups.

For easy cleanup of your paint tray, line the tray with a plastic bag before pouring in your paint. After the job's done, you can discard the bag without having to clean the roller tray.

To avoid having to clean a paint roller pan, press a sheet of aluminum foil into it before use. When you're finished, simply wrap up the foil and dispose of it.

Why buy new paint thinner when you can reuse the old? Here's how: Pour paint thinner into an empty coffee can. After you've cleaned your brushes, cover the can tightly and let it stand for several days. When paint from the brushes settles to the bottom as sediment, drain off the "clean" thinner into another can and store for reuse.

When you buy a new oil paint brush, soak it for a day in a can of linseed oil before using it. The brush will last longer and be easier to clean.

To clean a paint brush without making a mess of your hands, pour solvent into a strong, clear plastic bag, and insert the brush. Your hands will stay clean as you work the solvent into the bristles through the plastic.

If you store a partially used can of paint upside down, "skin" won't form on the surface of the paint. (Be sure the lid is tight.)

To clean a paint roller after use, roll it as dry as possible, first on the newly painted surface and then on several sheets of newspaper. Then slide the roller from its support and clean it with water or a solvent, depending on the type of paint used.

If you must leave a paint brush for a short time and don't want to clean it, wrap it in foil or a plastic bag to keep it soft and pliable. Put it in the freezer to save it for a longer time.

Leftover paint that is lumpy or contains shreds of paint "skin" can be strained through window screening.

To keep a brush as soft as new, clean it and then dip it in a final rinse containing fabric softener.

An empty coffee can with a plastic lid makes a perfect container for soaking brushes. Just make two slits in the center of the plastic lid to form an "X," push the brush handle up through the "X," and replace the lid. The lid seals the can so the solvent can't evaporate, and the brush is suspended without the bristles resting on the bottom.

White paint won't yellow if you stir in a drop of black paint.

A paste-type paint remover will remove paint spots from brick.

You can remove paint splatters from your hair by rubbing the spots with baby oil.

Wallpaper and Wallcoverings

If you're planning to paper all walls in a room, choose the least conspicuous area as your starting–finishing point. It's almost inevitable that the pattern won't match perfectly as you return to the start.

If there are stubborn grease spots on walls that you're going to paper, seal them with clear nail polish or shellac so that the grease won't soak through the new wallpaper.

To make wallpaper hanging easier, a right-handed person should work from left to right and a left-handed person from right to left.

Tint wallpaper paste slightly with food coloring so that you can see exactly where you've applied it.

Save time when applying wallpaper paste by using a short-napped paint roller.

To eliminate a bubble in wallpaper after the paste has dried, take a razor blade and slit the blister twice across its center, forming an "X." Peel back the slit's four tips, dab paste under them, press down, and smooth with a seam roller or the back of a spoon.

When papering over wall anchors or places where you plan to reposition shelves or pictures, insert toothpicks in holes left by screws or picture hooks. As you cover these sections, force the toothpick points through the paper to mark reinstallation points for screws or hooks.

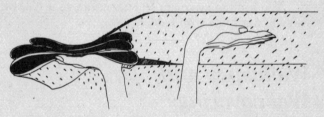

Wallpaper a ceiling with the strips positioned crosswise—they're shorter and more manageable. Accordion-fold each strip, pasted area against pasted area, and unfold it as you go along, supporting the paper with one hand and smoothing it onto the ceiling with the other.

After wallpapering a room where there'll be a lot of moisture—such as a kitchen or bathroom—cover all seams with clear varnish to help guard against peeling.

Save time when hanging the wallpaper itself by smoothing it with a clean, dry paint roller. If you attach the roller to a long handle, you can reach the ceiling or the tops of walls without climbing a ladder.

Use a squeegee to eliminate bubbles and wrinkles in vinyl wall coverings.

To eliminate a bubble in freshly hung wallpaper— while the paste is still wet—puncture the blister with a sharp needle or pin. Press the blister inward from its edges toward the puncture, squeezing out excess paste. Wipe this excess off with a damp sponge, and then press the area flat with a seam roller or the back of a spoon.

It's a good idea to save wallpaper for patching. Let it "weather" and fade at the same rate as the paper on the wall by taping a piece or two on a closet wall. If you do this, it will correspond in color density as well as pattern to the paper already on the wall.

If you lack wallpaper scraps for patching, try touching up the design in worn areas. Carefully use felt-tip pens to restore rubbed or faded colors.

If you don't have a seam roller to use to tame a loose wallpaper seam, rub the seam with the back of a spoon. White glue can substitute for wallpaper paste.

To repair a damaged wallpaper section, *tear* — don't cut—a patch from a piece that's been "weathered." Because less-defined torn edges blend imperceptibly with paper already on the wall, the patch will be virtually invisible. Note: Don't remove damaged wallpaper before placing a patch on it. Paste the patch directly over the damaged surface.

When preparing to remove old wallpaper, soak it first with very hot water applied with a paint roller; add a touch of detergent to the water to hasten the process.

If the paper is foil, or vinyl-coated, score its surface so water can penetrate to the backing.

When removing old wallpaper with a steamer, save the ceiling for last. As you work on the walls, steam rising from the applicator will loosen the ceiling paper. Much of it will start sagging from its own weight, and peeling it off will be easy.

If you're stapling fabric to a wall and you want to mask the staples at the top and bottom, glue a band of fabric—or even a wide, contrasting ribbon—over these seams. You also can cover the staples with molding strips.

When paneling a room, let the panels acclimate to the room's humidity for 48 hours before positioning them. This helps prevent them from being installed too tightly or too loosely.

When applying wood paneling to a wall you can attach panels directly to the studs. However, panels attached this way tend to give a little and are not as soundproof as those installed over either a plywood or a gypsum board backing.

When you're installing wood panels, first lean them against the wall as you think they should be placed. This gives you a chance to arrange the wood graining in the manner that pleases you most. When they're positioned the way you want them, number the panels for reference and proceed with the project.

Instead of carrying large wallboard sheets into the house and possibly damaging them when navigating awkward corners, measure and cut them to fit before bringing them inside.

When using a hand saw or a table saw to cut a wood panel, cut the panel with the face up. When using a hand power saw, cut the panel with the face down.

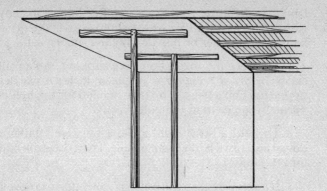

To save your arm muscles when installing ceiling wallboard, construct two "deadman" supports. These consist of 2 x 4s of the proper floor-to-ceiling length, including T-bars at their tops. They effortlessly support the panels while you do the final positioning and securing.

Do you want to discourage nails from "popping" out of wallboard? Drive them in in pairs, spaced 2 inches apart. Each strengthens the holding power of the other. If you're driving nails into a stud where two wallboard edges butt up against each other, stagger the double nailing on each side of the interface.

To help absorb noise, install acoustical tiles on doors to playrooms. You could also reduce noise in your home by using such tile to line the rooms or closets that house central heating and air conditioning units.

Wall Repairs and Ceramic Tile

A saucepan lid makes a good container for joint compound, since the lid's knob lets you hold the "bowl" easily during application. (When you've finished, make sure you rinse out the lid before any residue hardens.) Other easy-to-hold containers are a bathroom plunger or half of a hollow rubber ball.

To prevent a toggle bolt from slipping into a wall cavity before a hang-up is in place, insert a washer under the bolt's head. (The hole needed for the bolt is normally larger than the bolt's head.)

To hold a heavy bolt in a masonry wall, taper a dowel and drive it into a small hole. Then drive the bolt into the dowel.

If a screw hole in the wall has worn-down grooves, stuff the hole with a cotton ball soaked in white glue, and let it dry for 24 hours. You'll then be able to insert a screw securely using a screwdriver.

To patch a small hole in drywall you can use a tin can lid covered by a plaster patch. Thread a wire in and back out through two holes in the can lid, and then slide the lid behind the wall through horizontal slits cut out from each side of the hole. Pull the lid flat on the inside, and hold it in place while you apply plaster.

A beer can opener makes a good tool for cutting loose plaster out of a wall before patching a large crack. Use the pointed end of the opener to undercut and widen the opening.

It will be easier to fill a large hole in the wall if you first jam a piece of wallboard into the hole, and then mar the wallboard's surface so it's rough. The spackle will adhere tightly to the wallboard piece and won't sink in and require further applications.

It's best to fill wide cracks in plaster from the inside out, pressing fresh plaster in with a putty knife or a trowel.

Adding a tablespoon of white vinegar to the water when mixing patching plaster will keep the compound from drying too quickly, allowing you more time to work.

You'll be able to remove a damaged ceramic tile easily if you first drill a hole through its center and score an "X" across it with a glass cutter. Then chisel out the pieces.

To fit a ceramic tile around the stem of a shower pipe, cut the tile in half and then cut semicircles out of each half with tile nippers.

When replacing an individual ceramic wall tile, it helps to tape it securely to surrounding tiles until its mastic dries.

Hanging Pictures and Mirrors

Take the guesswork out of arranging several pictures on the wall. Spread a large sheet of wrapping paper or several taped-together newspapers on the floor and experiment with frame positions. When you decide on a pleasing grouping, outline the frames on the paper, tape the paper to the wall, and drive hooks through the paper into the wall. Then remove the paper and hang the pictures.

Sometimes a picture that was positioned correctly won't hang straight. Wrap masking tape around the wire on both sides of the hook so that the wire can't slip. Or install parallel nails and hooks a short distance apart; two hooks are better than one for keeping pictures in their places. Squares of double-faced tape affixed to the frame's two lower back corners also will keep pictures from moving. (If you don't have double-faced tape, make two loops with masking tape, sticky side out. Apply to each of the lower back corners and press the picture against the wall.)

Picture hanging can be frustrating if you simply try to "eyeball" the right spot to put the hook. Instead, place a picture exactly where you want it the first time with the following method: Cut a sheet of paper to the exact size of the frame. Position the pattern on the back of the picture, pull up taut the wire the picture will hang from, and mark the inverted "V" point on the pattern. Adjust the pattern on the wall, and then poke through it to mark the "V" point on the wall. If you nail the hook there, the picture will hang precisely where you wanted it.

If the picture isn't too heavy, another time-saving method is to hold the picture itself by its wire and decide where you want it positioned. Wet a fingertip and press it on the wall to mark the wire's inverted "V" point. The fingerprint mark will stay wet long enough for you to drive a nail and hook on target.

Don't lose a perfect picture grouping when you repaint a room—insert toothpicks in the hook holes and paint right over them; when the paint dries, remove the toothpicks and rehang your pictures.

To prevent a plaster wall from crumbling when driving in a nail and hook, first form an "X" over the nail spot with two strips of masking tape or transparent tape.

If you're hanging a picture from a molding but don't like the look of exposed picture wire, substitute nylon fishing line. The transparent nylon does a disappearing act that allows your picture to star on its own.

Hang heavy objects without special anchors by driving nails directly into the wooden studs behind walls. There are several ways to locate studs. You can tap a wall gently with your knuckles or a hammer. A wall sounds hollow between studs; solid on top of them. Or, move an electric razor (turned on) along a wall; a razor registers a different tone over studs. If nails were used to attach drywall to studs, a magnet will indicate the location of the nails, and, therefore, the studs.

When hanging a mirror with screws that go through mounting holes in the glass, don't tighten the screws all the way. Leave enough play to prevent the mirror from cracking if the wall shifts.

Hang mirrors to reflect *you* but not the sun; some mirror backings are adversely affected by direct sunlight.

Sometimes a picture that has been hanging for a while will leave darkish outlines on the wall because dust and dirt have collected against the frame. To prevent such build-up, allow better air circulation by holding pictures slightly away from the wall with thumb tacks pressed firmly into the backs of their frames. You can get the same result by fixing small tabs of self-sticking foam weather-stripping to the picture backing.

Outside Home Repairs

Roof Repairs

If there's an unfinished attic or crawl space below a leaky roof, finding the leak shouldn't be too hard. Climb into this space and look around with a flashlight—it's easier to see a leak in the semidark, so don't turn on a light. When you find the leak, outline the wet area with chalk. If possible, push a piece of wire up through the leaky spot, so that it protrudes from the roof. This makes it easier to find the leak when you're working outside.

If possible, repair shingles on a sunny day. A wet roof is dangerously slippery.

You can repair split shingles temporarily even if you don't have any flashing. Put a piece of cardboard in a plastic bag and then slide the bag under the shingles.

You don't have to replace a cracked asbestos shingle if all the pieces are still in place. Pull out the obstructing nails and slide a piece of roofing felt or roll roofing under the shingle until it is behind the cracks. Drill holes for the new nails needed, then drive in the nails gently. Cover the nail heads with roof cement.

If black roofing drips tar down on shingles when you're patching, soak a rough rag or brush in kerosene and scrub the stains off right away.

New asphalt shingles can be put down over old asphalt, wood, and roll roofing if it's only one or two layers. If it's in three layers, the old roofing must be stripped off. Cedar shakes, slate shingles, or tiles, however, must be taken off.

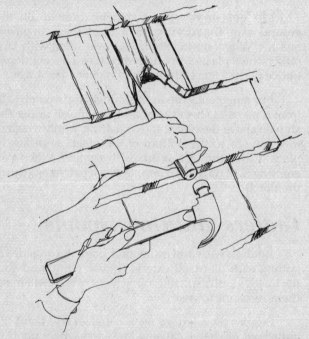

If you want to replace a damaged shake and it doesn't come out easily, split it into several pieces with a hammer and chisel. Remove the pieces and extract the nails.

If the deck under old shingles is spaced sheathing, begin at the ridge so that debris does not fall through the spaces into the house.

To avoid having a new-looking, unweathered patch in repaired shingles or shakes, take replacements from an inconspicuous area of the house and use new shingles or shakes on that spot.

To make it easier to slide a new shingle up into place, round the back corners slightly with a sharp utility knife. Then lift the corners of the overlapping shingles and drive in a roofing nail at each corner.

Do not store asphalt shingles directly on the ground or on the roof overnight. Stack them on pieces of 2 x 4. When storing shingles, cover them with tarp rather than plastic, because moisture can condense under plastic. Stack shingles no higher than 4 feet.

For emergency repair of a shingle, cut a patch to fit from a piece of sheet metal and slip it well under the shingle above the one you're repairing. Apply a coat of roof cement to the bottom of the patch, and tack in place. Cover the tack heads with cement. When you come back to do a more permanent repair later, pry up the patch.

Gutters and Downspouts

For best wear and protection, paint the outsides of gutters with oil-based exterior house paint, and coat the insides with asphalt roofing paint, which will make them resistant to rust.

Never rest a ladder on a gutter. It will bend the gutter out of shape, causing low spots where pools of water will collect when it rains.

When cleaning gutters, inspect each hanger for bent straps and popped nails as you work your way along the gutter. If the house has a fascia or board trim, check the gutter's alignment with it. The gutter should rest firmly against the fascia for maximum support.

Clean gutters by hand, then hose them down after you've removed the debris. This flushes out the remnant and gives you an opportunity to observe the flow of water and see low spots or improper pitch.

Check the nails or screws in the straps holding the downspout to your house. These can work themselves loose with use or age, or when a downspout has been used as a ladder support.

If you are replacing only a section or two of gutter, take a cross-sectional piece with you when buying a new one. You'll need an exact match of shape and metal.

Using a spray-on auto undercoating is a quick and easy way to repair your rain gutters. If you notice any gaps in the gutter, simply spray. If you have to patch a small hole, put a piece of screen wire over the hole and then spray on the undercoating.

To keep downspouts clear, flush them frequently with a garden hose. If necessary, remove stubborn clogs with a plumber's snake.

When installing a new gutter, get someone to help with lifting the gutter sections. Positioning long sections cannot be done by one person.

Concrete Work

When you're pouring concrete steps, be sure to use solid objects as fillers; hollow objects buried in concrete—pieces of pipe, for example—have a tendency to float to the surface.

A smooth concrete surface is a hazard on outdoor steps. After the concrete has settled, but while it is still workable, run a stiff broom across the steps to roughen the surface.

If a hollow glass block in your garage wall breaks, clean the opening and soak some pieces of brick. Put the pieces into the opening and pack the hole solidly with concrete mix. You must use brick or the mix will fall out.

Make drilling in masonry easier by making a pilot hole with a masonry nail at the exact spot where you want to drill.

If you put sand on top of asphalt sealer it will prevent the sealer from sticking to your shoes.

You can prevent wooden forms from sticking to concrete by painting the parts that will be in contact with the cement with oil.

An old metal Venetian blind slat can be used as a finishing trowel on small concrete jobs.

Siding Repairs and Maintenance

Cracked, warped, or loose siding should be repaired as soon as you notice it. Water works its way through such defects into the interior wall where rotting can take place undetected. If you don't have time for a thorough repair, seal splits with oil-based caulking compound and clamp them together by driving nails and clinching them over the boards. This is an effective short-term expedient.

Never caulk when the temperature falls below 50°F. For an emergency job in cold weather, use polybutane cord.

The best time to caulk is when painting the house. Apply primer to the seams first, then caulk. (Primer helps the caulking stick.) Allow the caulking to cure for a couple of days, then apply a finish coat. Be sure to use a compound that will take paint.

If you caulk in very hot weather and the caulking gets runny, place it in the refrigerator for an hour or two.

To remove white powdery surfaces on brick or concrete surfaces, go over them with a stiff brush. Wet the surface with a weak 5 percent solution of muriatic acid and water, leave the solution on for 5 minutes, then brush the wall and rinse immediately with clear water. Work a 4-foot-square section at a time.

When mixing acid and water always add the acid to the water, *never* vice versa. Put on goggles, gloves, and an apron before mixing, and leave them on until after you rinse off.

To remove mildew from house siding, scrub the surface with a bleach and water solution (1 cup of bleach to 1 gallon of warm water). Flush the area with clear water and allow it to dry thoroughly before painting.

Other Outside Projects

If you plan to install a skylight, position it on the northern slope of your roof. Because a skylight can really heat up a room on a sunny day, make sure the attic is well ventilated.

If you camouflage telephone poles or clothes lines with black paint, they seem to disappear.

When installing an antenna, position it where it cannot fall across a power line.

If water is seeping into your basement, inspect to see if water collects on the ground near the foundation of the house. Soil should slope away from a house, so if the ground is level or slopes in toward the foundation, you may be able to solve your seepage problem by regrading the soil so it slopes properly.

To keep water from collecting where a paved area meets the foundation of your home, undercut the joint, fill it with mortar, and then shape the mortar into a smooth curve with the back of a spoon.

Help prevent ice dams by installing insulation between the rafters in your attic. Use insulation with a vapor barrier and leave air space between the vapor barrier and roof boards under an underhang. The insulation should be 6 inches deep.

You can also prevent ice dams by providing ventilation for the attic through the soffit vent between lookout beams, which can be located by nail heads in the soffit.

Chimney Repairs

The chimney in your home should be inspected each year just before the cold season to reduce the chance of fire and to increase efficiency.

You'll see more if you inspect the chimney from the top. On a bright day use a mirror to reflect sunlight down into the chimney. If you can't look down a chimney, inspect it with a strong flashlight and mirror from a fireplace or from the flue opening for a stove pipe.

If the chimney has crumbling mortar, be careful as you chip away cracked, loose mortar in preparation for tuckpointing or remortaring. A chimney in poor condition could topple at any time.

Tools and Ladders

To keep your hands free while you're making repairs, make a holster for the nails and screws you'll need. Take a paper cup and make two vertical slits in it about an inch apart; the slits should be wide enough to let you slip your belt through them.

When working on a steeply sloped roof, keep your tools on a sheet of plastic foam. That way they won't slide off.

Need a place to hold your hammer when you're on the roof? Attach a shower curtain ring to your belt and slip the hammer through it.

When using an aluminum ladder, watch out for power lines: aluminum *conducts* electricity.

If you're planning to work on a ladder extended to its full height, gain stability by lashing the bottom rung to two stakes driven into the ground under and to the sides of the ladder.

Before climbing up a ladder test the bottom rung to make sure the ladder is solidly footed.

The best way for a lone worker to raise a ladder is to pin its feet against the base of the house and push the ladder up from the other end, hand over hand, until it is upright.

Keep your hips within the ladder's rails. Extend the top two rungs higher than the place where you're working. The ladder should always extend up above the roof.

Make sure your ladder has firm support at the top. Placing it against a window sash or close to an edge means a slight shift could cause you to fall.

Water System

If you're shutting down your house for the winter, turn off the house water supply at the underground street valve.

Here's a fast way to clean the house water pipes of water when shutting down a house. After the water heater has been drained and everything else is empty, there may be water left in low spots in the horizontal mains. Just stick the end of a running air compressor hose into an opened outdoor hose faucet. The air pressure will shoot the water out wherever there is an opening. When only air comes out, you're done. This beats crawling under the house to drain the pipes.

When shutting down your water system, open all the faucets and outdoor hose spigots to drain. Flush the toilet and sponge out remaining water from tank. Drain or blow water out of fixture traps, including the toilet. After removing all the tap water from the sink and lavatory traps, fill the traps with a mixture of a little kerosene and a lot of denatured alcohol. Kerosene will keep the alcohol from evaporating.

Workshop, Basement, and Garage

General Shop

Loosen a stubborn screw, bolt, or nut with a shot of penetrating oil. If you don't have oil, use hydrogen peroxide, white vinegar, kerosene, or household ammonia. Should these prove ineffective, heat the metal with an iron, rap it sharply with a hammer while it's still hot, and try again to loosen it.

You can work most rusted bolts loose by pouring a carbonated beverage on them.

If a bolt repeatedly loosens due to vibrations, coat the threads with fingernail polish and reinsert it. It won't loosen again. And if you need to remove it, you can break the seal with a little effort.

You can prevent a knot in nylon rope from working loose by holding it briefly over a small flame. The heat will melt and bond the fibers.

Avoid burning your fingers when lighting a pilot light with a short match. Simply clamp the match in an alligator clip at the end of a straightened coat hanger.

You can use a coping saw blade to remove a broken-off key from a lock. Slide the blade in beside the key, turn it toward the key so its teeth sink into the key's soft brass, and then pull the blade out along with the key fragment.

Dipping the ends of a rope in shellac will keep them from unraveling.

To prevent metal tubing from denting when sawing it, insert a round dowel that fits the tube's interior tightly.

To hide a screw head, drill a counterbored hole, seat the screw, glue a piece of doweling into the counterbore, and sand it flush.

As an aid in measuring lumber or pipe, paint lines a foot apart on a concrete floor.

If you're out of penetrating oil, you can substitute hydrogen peroxide, lemon juice, or kerosene.

An old nylon stocking makes an effective strainer if you're out of cheesecloth.

For easy workshop measuring, fasten a yardstick to the edge of your workbench. Cut keyhole slots in the yardstick so you can remove it when you need it elsewhere.

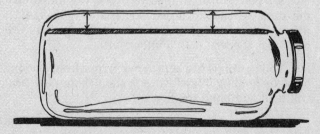

If you don't have a carpenter's level, you can substitute a tall, straight-sided jar with a lid. Fill the jar three-quarters full with water. Lay it on its side on the surface you're testing—when the water is level, the surface is, too.

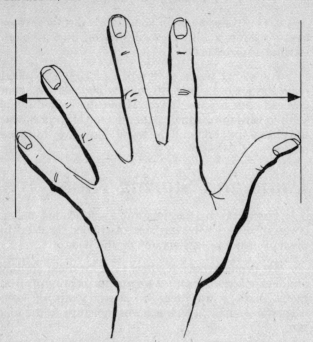

If you know the exact width of your hand with thumb and fingers spread, you can make rough measurements without using a ruler or tape measure.

In your workshop, use a pocketed shoebag for such items as cans. The bag holds more and takes up less space than a shelf.

An empty soft-drink carton makes a convenient kit for holding and carrying lubricants.

If you need more workbench storage space, slide an old dresser under the bench and use the drawers for storage.

Empty hand-cream jars are great storage containers for nails. The greasy film left on the sides of the jar will prevent the nails from rusting.

To keep the pores of your hands dirt- or grease-free, wipe on a thin coat of shaving cream before starting a messy task.

You won't waste time when picking up spilled nails, screws, or tacks if you collect them with a magnet covered with a paper towel. When the spilled items snap toward the magnet, gather the towel corners over the pieces and then pull the towel "bag" away from the magnet.

Using and Storing Tools

To transform a hammer into a soft-headed mallet, cover the head with the sort of rubber tip used to prevent furniture legs scratching the floor.

To protect tools, it's best to store them so they aren't exposed to moisture. Keep a thin coating of oil on metal parts, wrap them in plastic wrap, or keep carpenter's chalk, which absorbs moisture, in the tool box.

To sharpen scissors, use them to slice up several pieces of sandpaper.

A piece of garden hose, slit open, is a handy protective cover for the teeth of a hand saw between projects.

To guard the teeth of circular saw blades when not in use, store the blades in record album covers. You could even store them in an ordinary record rack in your workshop.

To prevent a screwdriver from slipping, rub chalk on the blade.

If you hang tools on pegboard walls, outline each tool with an artist's brush so you'll know at a glance where each tool goes. You'll also know when a tool hasn't been replaced.

If you want to remind yourself to unplug an electric drill when changing accessories, fasten the chuck key near the plug end of the cord.

Keep screwdrivers handy—slide the blades through the mesh in plastic berry baskets nailed to the shop wall.

Snow won't stick to your shovel if you give the shovel a coat of floor wax.

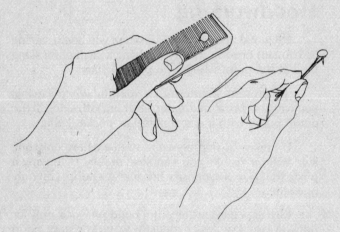

Don't take a chance of hitting a thumb or finger when hammering a small brad, tack, or nail. Slip the fastener between the teeth of a pocket comb; the comb holds the nail while you hold the comb. A bobby pin or a paper clip can be used the same way as a comb.

To retard moisture and rust, keep mothballs with your tools. If rust spots appear, rub them away with a typewriter eraser.

Here's a do-it-yourself rust-preventive coating for tools, outdoor furniture, and other metal objects: Combine ¼ cup of lanolin and 1 cup of petroleum jelly in a double boiler over low heat. Stir until the mixture melts and blends completely, and then remove from heat and pour into a clean jar, letting the mixture cool partially. Use the mixture while it's still warm, and don't wipe it off—just let it dry on the object. If there's any extra, cover it tightly, and rewarm it before you use it again.

Paint all tool handles with an unusual, bright color, or wrap reflective tape around them; they'll be easy to identify if borrowed or left in the wrong place.

Woodworking

Plywood frequently splits when you begin sawing it. You can prevent this by applying a strip of masking tape at the point where you plan to start.

To prevent splintering or splitting when sawing, you can also prescore the top layer on both sides, at the cutoff point, with a sharp chisel or pocket knife.

If you're buying plywood to use where only one side will be visible, you can save money by buying a piece that is less expensive because it's perfect on only one side.

Use expensive waterproof bond plywood only for outside use. Use less expensive water-resistant bond plywood when panels will be exposed to weather infrequently. And use relatively inexpensive dry bond plywood when panels will be used indoors.

You can saw a board into almost perfectly equal lengths without measuring it. Simply balance it on a single sawhorse. When the board stops wobbling the center will be the point where the board touches the crossbar of the sawhorse.

To make any sawing task smoother and easier, lubricate a saw's blade frequently by running a bar of soap or a candle stub over its sides.

To prevent a saw from binding when ripping a long board, hold the initial cut open with a nail or wedge. Move the nail or wedge down the cut as you continue to saw.

Saws cut more easily *across* the grain than with it. In ripping cuts there's a tendency for the blade to follow the grain, rather than a marked or scribed line, so watch carefully when making rip cuts or the cut might turn out wavy.

To prevent dimpling a wood surface when removing a nail with a hammer, protect the surface with a small block of wood or a shim; this, incidentally, will also increase your leverage.

To extract a nail without widening its hole or denting surrounding stock, use long-nose pliers and roll the pliers in your hand.

Check that wood is perfectly smooth after sanding by covering your hand with a nylon stocking and rubbing it over the surface. You'll be able to detect any rough spots that remain.

Sandpaper clogs fast, and usually before it's worn out. You can clean clogged sandpaper and give it new life by vacuuming it or rubbing a fine-bristled brush back and forth across its grit.

When gluing two pieces of wood together, position the grain in the same direction. If the pieces are crossgrained and later swell due to moisture absorption, the joint will pull apart.

When you drill through any kind of wood a certain amount of splintering will occur at the breakout point. (This is true regardless of the type of bit used, since wood has a composition that causes it to fracture rather than break.) You can prevent this breakout splintering by backing the stock with a piece of scrap.

Whenever there's danger of splitting a narrow section of wood with a screw, predrill a hole. Then the wood won't crack when you insert the screw.

Tack rags will last longer if they're stored in an airtight container to keep them from drying out. Airtight storage also prevents spontaneous combustion. (This safety tip applies equally well to other rags, coveralls, work gloves, and any other clothes that might absorb flammable oils and solvents.)

Though a hacksaw is designed to cut metal, the thin blade is well suited for cutting small pieces of wood accurately.

A plastic playing card or credit card can serve as a scraper for removing excess wood filler from a surface that you are repairing.

A salt shaker makes a good applicator for distributing pumice evenly on a wood surface.

Basement

You will have better daytime visibility in the basement if you paint window wells, basement walls, and basement ceilings white to reflect more outside light.

To guard against tracking dust or sawdust upstairs, carpet the basement steps. The nap of the carpet will brush dust or sawdust off the soles of your shoes.

If you have a moisture problem in your basement, you need to know whether the cause is seepage or condensation. To determine which of these causes applies, tape a hand mirror against a wall in the middle of a damp spot and leave it overnight. If the mirror is fogged the next morning, condensation is the cause of your moisture problem.

To get rid of condensation, either air the basement frequently or use the opposite approach —keep the basement doors closed and install storm windows in the basement to keep moisture out.

If basement moisture turns out to be seepage, you'll probably need professional help; in either case, however, it helps to wrap exposed cold-water pipes with nonsweat insulation and install a dehumidifier.

Garage

Luminous stripes painted on the rear garage wall can help you center your car when parking.

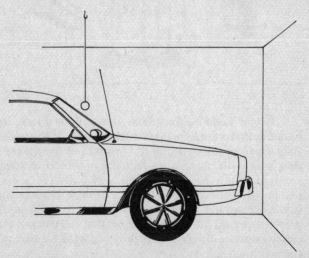

If you never are quite sure when to stop when you pull into your garage, suspend a ball on a string from the garage ceiling to act as a parking guide. Hang the ball so that it almost touches the windshield at eye level when you are seated at the steering wheel. When you drive in, stop just before the ball touches the windshield.

A "padded" garage can help you avoid scratching your car when pulling in and out. Attach sections of inner tube to both sides of the entranceway, if that is your problem area, or anywhere else that there's a danger of scratching the car.

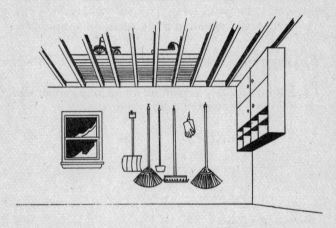

If you need to maximize garage floor space, try hanging items such as rakes and shovels on the walls. Gain more room by filling the top half of the garage's rear wall with shelves or cabinets in which to stash small tools, automotive supplies, and garden accessories. Position these cabinets high enough to allow the hood of your car to fit underneath. Overhead, lay a platform across the ceiling joists so that you can put the space between the ceiling and roof to work for storage, too.

Maximize garage floor space by painting white lines on the floor to outline parking areas for bicycles, the lawn mower, and other large objects. Then they'll be out of the way when you want to park the car.

Save space on your garage floor by stashing storm windows or screens overhead in a simple storage rack attached to existing ceiling joists.

To keep the garage floor free from grease and oil spots, place a drip pan under the car. Use a cookie sheet filled with cat litter, and replace the litter when it's saturated. Or cut a piece of corrugated cardboard to fit the cookie sheet and change it as necessary.

If you need a drip pan larger than a cookie sheet, fashion one from aluminum foil stapled to a piece of corrugated cardboard.

Garage floor oil and grease spots can be cleaned with paint thinner. Apply thinner and cover overnight with cat litter, dry Portland cement, or sand, then sweep. Repeat if necessary.

Some automotive oil spots can be lifted with baking soda or cornmeal. Sprinkle on and sweep off. Repeat as necessary.

As a last resort, try removing a stain on the garage floor with full-strength laundry bleach.

If all else fails, you can camouflage garage floor drippings with paint. Apply a black stripe the width of the space between the car's tires. The stripe doubles as a parking guide.

To avoid damaging your car doors after you've driven into the garage, staple inner-tube sections, foam rubber, carpet scraps, or rubber mats to the garage walls where doors might hit when opened.

To soften the blow in case you accidentally collide with the garage's rear wall when parking, cushion the wall with an old tire hung at bumper height.

If your wooden garage door is hard to open, it could be because it is not completely painted or sealed and so has swollen. (An unpainted door can bind at the edges and seem heavy.) To remedy this, let the door dry out thoroughly over several dry days, and then seal it by painting all surfaces, including edges.

Saving Energy in the Home

Cutting Heating and Cooling Costs

To check the efficiency of the heating system in a home you're thinking of buying, change the thermostat setting—raise it if it's cold outside and lower it if it's warm—and then see how fast the room heats up or cools down. It should take no more than half an hour for the home to reach the desired temperature.

Periodically cleaning the squirrel-cage-type blower in a forced-air heating system will improve its efficiency and lower the system's operating cost. A vacuum cleaner hose attachment and a stiff brush are effective cleaning tools for this purpose.

Your heating system will operate at peak efficiency only if it's clean, so regular maintenance means savings on fuel bills.

For each degree you set your thermostat above 70°F, you can expect a 3 percent rise in energy costs. For most people, a 65°F daytime setting and a 55°F nighttime setting is acceptable.

It takes less energy to run a thermostatically controlled electric blanket than it does to maintain daytime thermostat settings throughout the sleeping hours.

Exercise caution in setting low indoor thermostat temperatures. Older people may require temperatures above 65°F to protect them from hypothermia, a possibly fatal drop in body temperature. People with circulatory problems or those taking certain types of drugs may also be vulnerable. In such instances, ask your doctor about recommended winter and summer thermostat settings.

Reduce the thermostat setting before you go to bed at night; cutting back for several hours will measurably decrease fuel consumption.

To avoid having a thermostat turn the heat on or off when it's not necessary, make sure it doesn't misinterpret the true warmth of your home. This can happen if the thermostat is positioned in a drafty area, placed on a cold outside wall or near a fireplace, or installed too near a heat-producing appliance such as a TV set or a lamp.

Take advantage of the fact that a large group of people generates heat—reduce the thermostat setting when you're entertaining a crowd.

A portable hair dryer can be helpful in checking where doors or windows need additional weatherstripping. Move the air stream along the interface between a door and its frame or a sash and its frame. Have someone on the other side of the door or window follow the dryer's movements with his or her hands. Where heat is felt leaking through, you need a patch job.

Next time a banging radiator is driving you crazy, make a quick check with a level. The radiator should slope down on one side, toward the pipes and the boiler. If it doesn't, you can stop the banging by propping up the outside legs.

Turn the thermostat to its lowest setting if you won't be at home for a few days. You can turn off the heating system completely if there's no danger of pipes freezing while you're away.

Walk around the house with a candle on a cold windy day to see where cold may be entering around doors and windows.

Save on heating costs and stay comfortable in cold weather by dressing to retain body heat. Layer your clothing: wear lightweight basic garments, such as a shirt or blouse or short-sleeved sweater, covered by heavier garments, such as a sweater vest, and topped with a warm jacket or sweater jacket. If you become too warm you can adjust your own body thermostat by taking off a layer.

Many types of weatherstripping must be installed with nails. You can use any type of hammer, but a magnetic tack hammer works best for driving small brads in cramped areas.

To speed the installation of weatherstripping, try stapling instead of nailing it.

Keeping your home well caulked is one of the best ways to save energy. When you caulk, make sure joints are thoroughly dry—you can dry deep crevices with a cloth stretched over the blade of a putty knife, or with a blast of hot air from a hair dryer.

When caulking several joints, start with the smallest joint and recut the tube's nozzle as necessary for successively larger joints.

Loose-fitting windows can lose heat up to five times faster than windows that fit properly. To check a window for air leaks, feel around the edges for air movement on a windy day. Or light a candle or match and move it around the edges; if the flame flickers, heat is being lost and weatherstripping is needed. Weather-stripping is also needed if ice or condensation builds up on a storm window; this is a clue that air is seeping around the interior window.

A room will stay warmer in cold weather if curtains fit tightly against the window's frame so that warm room air doesn't move across the cold window surface. A fixed valance at the top and sides of the curtains will help, and so will weighting or fastening the curtains at the bottom.

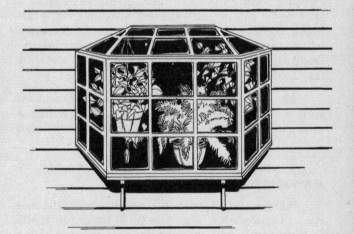

Installing a window greenhouse in one or more of your house's south-facing windows is an unusual (and effective) way to gain extra heat for your home in winter, to reduce the loss of heat to the outdoors in the evening, and, of course, to provide an encouraging environment for plants. Such greenhouses can fill even east or west windows if you install reflectors to catch more of the sun's rays.

If you plan to install new shades or blinds to help keep your home warm, consider mounting them outside the frames. If they're installed inside window frames air can leak along the edges, but outside mountings help reduce the flow of air against cold window glass.

Solar reflective films applied over your windows in warm-weather months will reduce the amount of light and, therefore, of heat that enters your home.

A simple strategy like keeping your windows sparkling clean in winter can help warm your home. Spotless window glass lets in more sunlight than grimy panes.

To maintain your home's temperature, latch the windows—instead of merely closing them—for a tighter seal.

It's best to remove window screens before winter arrives because fine-mesh screen can reduce by up to 20 percent the amount of warming sunlight entering your home.

During winter months, cooking foods slowly in the oven at low temperatures will provide extra heat to help warm the house.

Hot bath water will help keep your bathroom warm in cold weather months if you leave it to cool before draining the tub. The water will also add humidity to contribute to the comfort of your home.

Aluminum foil placed behind a radiator helps to reflect heat into the room. Tape a piece of foil to the wall directly behind the radiator, shiny side out; use duct tape all around the edges.

Because a great deal of heat is conducted through large, overhead garage doors, a significant amount of heat can escape from a home that has an attached garage but no insulation between the house and the garage. An insulated and weatherstripped garage door, therefore, can save you money, even if the garage is unheated.

Odors emitted by a central air conditioner usually indicate condensate drain fungus. You can eliminate the smell by pouring laundry bleach into the condensate pan to kill the fungus.

Since cold air falls, you'll get better air circulation from a room air conditioner if you aim its vents upward.

If you have a forced air heating system but use window air conditioning units, be sure to close the heating system vents so cold air doesn't escape through the ducts and fall to the basement.

To keep air conditioning to a minimum, be sure you're not overheating your home needlessly. Draw your draperies against direct sunlight, and switch off lighting fixtures when you're not in the room. If you have the facilities, consider barbecuing outdoors so that you can keep the kitchen cool.

If you install your air conditioner with the thermostat away from heat-producing appliances and direct sunlight, it won't "think" the room is warmer than it really is and work overtime. So place any outdoor portions of your unit or a central unit where they'll receive the least direct sunlight.

Using a patio cover will reduce the load your air conditioning unit bears in the summertime. The cover shields the concrete from sunlight that would otherwise reflect and radiate into your home. Conversely, removing the cover in winter months lets you take advantage of the heat generated by reflected sunlight.

Keep furnishings away from air conditioning vents so that the cold air can circulate freely.

Save on energy costs by turning off your air conditioning unit when you leave home. If you're gone every day, install a timer control to keep the unit off until shortly before you return in the evening. (You can manually override the time when you're at home.)

Awnings and canopies can keep your home cooler in the summertime.

Wood Stoves and Fireplaces

Have the elbows, joints, flue, and chimney of a stovepipe thoroughly cleaned once a year.

When installing a woodburning stove, select a brand made of steel or cast iron for safety. Be sure that the stove carries a label indicating that it's been tested for reliability.

When purchasing a used stove, carefully check the condition of the hinges, grates, and draft louvers, and the sturdiness of the legs. Reject any stove with cracks.

A stove should be installed only over a fireproof material such as brick or stone, or an asbestos plate covered with metal made especially for the purpose.

Keep easily flammable materials such as newspapers and magazines, wooden furniture, and firewood logs at a safe distance from your stove.

Before operating a newly installed stove, read the instruction manual for safety tips, or contact your local fire department for safety specifications on the stovepipe and flue.

Never use lighter fluid or other flammable liquids to start a fire. Place kindling wood and crumpled pieces of newspaper under your logs to help fan the flames.

The only material suitable for burning in a wood stove is dry, seasoned firewood.

Always extinguish the fire in a wood stove before leaving the house or before going to bed at night.

Empty cardboard milk cartons make wonderful kindling for fires. So do candle stubs.

When burning fireplace logs, sprinkle salt on them periodically. You can reduce soot by two-thirds by doing this.

To make newspaper logs, coat a 3-foot dowel, or a section of broomstick, with paste wax. When the wax dries, buff it to a smooth finish. Place a newspaper on a large flat surface; hold the dowel firmly at each end, and roll sheets of paper onto the dowel as tightly as you can. (Tightly rolled logs burn much longer than loosely rolled ones.) Continue to roll paper onto the dowel until the roll is 3–3½ inches in diameter. Carefully holding the paper in place, fasten the log firmly at each end and in the center with thin wire. Slide the dowel out of the roll, and repeat to make as many logs as needed. Two to three thick newspaper sections make one log.

To make a dry fire extinguisher, pour 6 pounds of fine sand into a large container and add 2 pounds of baking soda. Stir the mixture thoroughly. Keep the container in your shop, garage, or kitchen. This mixture can be sprinkled directly on small oil, grease, and petroleum product fires.

Add a curved-tube convection heater to your fireplace to draw more heat from the fire into the room, instead of letting it escape up the flue.

A curved-tube heater that has a blower unit can double the amount of heat thrown into a room from your fireplace. Be sure to select one that's big enough to fill the opening.

When you're not using the fireplace, be sure you're not losing heated air through the chimney; remember to keep the damper in the fireplace closed except when a fire is burning.

A fireplace draws air from the house to keep the fire going, so if your furnace is operating and warming up the air while the fireplace is going, the net effect is that you're paying to heat air that is going right up the chimney. The best way to correct this problem is to install an outside air vent directly in front of the fireplace. The fireplace will then operate on outside air instead of on your heated air. It's also a good idea to close the doors to the room where the fireplace is being used.

Ceiling Fans

With an old-fashioned ceiling fan, avoid using a light dimmer switch as a variable speed control. A light dimmer switch can't handle the electrical load involved. Use only a speed control and lighting-fixture outlet designed for your specific brand of fan.

Don't install an old-fashioned ceiling fan too close to curtains; the blades could rip them away from the window.

Never install an old-fashioned ceiling fan on a ceiling that's less than 8 feet high, since the blades twirl about a foot lower. If the ceiling is too low, the blades are close enough to head level to be dangerous.

Make sure that the ceiling fan in your bedroom doesn't hang so low that you hit it every time you raise your arms to take off your sweater.

Energy Efficient
Use of Appliances

About 95 percent of the energy used by a washing machine goes into heating the water. A machine with a cold rinse cycle will save some of that energy and cost you less to operate.

You'll use less electricity when running your washing machine if you select the shortest cycle and the coldest water temperature appropriate for the type of fabric being washed. Using the right amount of detergent is important, too, since oversudsing can overwork the machine.

Because some fabrics require less drying time than others, try to run loads of similar fabrics in your clothes dryer.

Save energy by drying clothes in consecutive loads; the dryer retains heat from one load to the next.

Position a refrigerator where there's plenty of air circulation. A refrigerator uses more energy when located near a stove or a heating vent.

To lengthen the life of your refrigerator and increase the unit's efficiency, periodically vacuum the dust that collects on the coils at the back of the refrigerator.

Color television sets use almost twice as much electricity as black and white sets. If you have both, it will cost less to watch a black and white movie on a black and white set.

If you want a mini-TV that's truly portable, make sure it operates on both AC or DC current. However, if you don't plan to use it outdoors, consider getting a larger set, with a larger screen, that operates on household current only. Though still portable, it'll cost less than a true mini.

Before you buy any TV set, study the picture it produces under lighting conditions similar to those of the room in which you'll watch at home. If you're not satisfied with the picture, look at other sets.

Saving Energy in the Kitchen

Sensible use of pots and pans can save energy when you use your range. Fit the pot or pan to the burner; a small pot or pan on a large element wastes heat, and a large pot on a small element is inefficient.

Whenever practical, use small cooking appliances, such as electric frying pans, instead of your range. These small units are energy-efficient and throw less heat into your kitchen.

To conserve energy when using the stovetop units on an electric range, turn off burners a short time before cooking is complete. With electric burners, the cooking process often continues for as long as 5 minutes after the burner is turned off.

You'll use less energy when cooking if you cook with as little water as possible; small amounts heat more quickly.

Another energy-saving tip: Put a lid on the pan you're using because water boils faster when covered.

To save on heat costs, don't turn on an element or burner until the pot or pan is on the stove. If you're going to simmer, turn down the heat as soon as the liquid reaches the boiling stage. Adjust the setting to just keep the contents boiling; a higher setting wastes energy. Copper and stainless steel cookware usually require lower heat settings than aluminum cookware.

It's important to keep pan bottoms clean because a layer of soot decreases heating efficiency on any type of stove. Shiny pans are particularly efficient on an electric range.

To save energy when using your oven, don't preheat it unless required. If you must preheat, put the food in as soon as the oven reaches the desired temperature. Cook as many items as possible at one time. Also, if you have a double oven, use the smaller one whenever possible.

Since a great deal of heat escapes each time you open the oven to examine what's cooking, you can conserve energy by minimizing the number of times you peek at the food inside. (During the summer, heat that escapes when you open the oven also puts extra strain on your air conditioner.)

Try cooking food items in the oven-usable paperboard containers in which they're packaged. You'll save from 10 to 20 percent of the oven energy normally required. The containers withstand temperatures up to 400°F. Don't, however, try to reuse them.

A self-cleaning oven will use less energy if you start the cleaning cycle right after cooking, when the oven will already be on its way to the high temperature needed for cleaning.

To conserve refrigerator and/or freezer energy by minimizing loss of cold air, plan ahead and put in or take out as many items as possible each time you open the unit.

Make sure your refrigerator is standing on the level; if it isn't, it may be working harder than necessary.

If you notice water standing in the bottom of your refrigerator, there may be an air leak around the door. To test the gasket, close the door on a dollar bill. If the bill pulls out easily, the gasket needs replacing.

A good way to keep your freezer from expending too much energy is to put it at the lowest setting that keeps ice cream firm. If your ice cream is rock-hard, the setting is unnecessarily high.

If you have a frostfree freezer, keep all liquids tightly covered. Uncovered liquids evaporate, form frost, and cause a frostfree system to work harder.

Energy Efficient Home Lighting

To save energy, convert incandescent fixtures to fluorescent wherever practical. Fluorescent tubes illuminate more efficiently than incandescent bulbs.

To make sure that bulbs in remote places (attic, basement, garage, or closets, for example), aren't left burning, install automatic switches that shut off the lights in a room when the door is closed.

Another way to monitor lights in remote areas of the house is to install a switch with a red pilot indicator. When the red light glows, you'll know lights in the basement, garage, etc. have inadvertently been left on. These remote switches are available from hardware stores.

Three-way bulbs, like dimmers, let you adjust lighting intensity to your needs and can save electrical energy. If a fixture won't take a three-way bulb, reduce the size (wattage) if you need the bulb only for general light.

If you install bright security lights, consider controlling them with a photoelectric cell or timer that turns the lights on at dusk and off at dawn; this means you can avoid burning the lights unnecessarily.

It is important that light fixtures be kept clean, because a dusty or dirty light fixture will absorb light, decreasing the amount of illumination reaching areas where it's needed. A dirty fixture may therefore prompt family members to turn on additional lights that shouldn't be necessary.

Getting rid of a decorative outdoor gas lamp can save you money in energy costs. However, if you need outdoor light for visibility or security, consider converting a gas lamp to electricity. This will reduce energy consumption considerably, especially if the lamp is turned on only when necessary.

To save energy, use one large bulb rather than several smaller ones. It requires six 25-watt bulbs to produce the light of a single 100-watt bulb.

If you turn a three-way bulb to the lowest level while watching television you'll both save energy and reduce glare in the room.

White or light-colored lampshades capitalize on the light produced by lamp bulbs. With such shades, a lower-wattage bulb can produce the same amount of light as a higher-wattage bulb screened with a dark-colored shade.

Fifty-watt reflector floodlights are recommended for directional lamps such as pole or spot lamps. They require half the wattage of standard 100-watt bulbs, yet provide nearly the same amount of illumination.

The smallest diameter recommended for a lampshade is 16 inches. Anything smaller will waste electricity by not diffusing enough light to be functional.

In high-intensity portable lamps, you can substitute 25-watt reflector bulbs for the 40-watt bulbs normally used; you'll get approximately the same illumination while consuming less energy.

Energy Efficient Water Use

Increase the efficiency of your water heater by spreading the family's baths, dishwashing, and laundry throughout the day. Also consider showering rather than tub bathing because a short shower consumes 4 to 8 gallons of hot water, while a bath uses 20 gallons or more.

Another way to make your water heater still more efficient is to use cold rather than hot water for washing clothes. Many modern fabrics and detergents are actually designed for cold-water washing.

A moderate temperature setting further increases a water heater's efficiency, since the "normal" setting, usually about 140°F, supplies all the heat most people need.

If your water heater is warm to the touch, it is not well insulated and is wasting energy. Wrap insulation around the tank to solve the problem.

If you have a swimming pool, economize on your water bills by filling your swimming pool with rain water. Attach an elbow connection to the gutter spout on your house and run a pipe from the elbow connection to your pool.

To prevent water from cooling as it travels to your plumbing fixtures, wrap hot water pipes with insulating material.

Sediment buildup can slow your water heater's recovery rate. If you notice a marked drop in recovery time, drain the sediment from the tank.

To prevent sediment from building up in your water heater, drain the heater periodically. Perform this maintenance step early in the morning, before any one has used hot water and disturbed the water in the tank.

If you have an electric water heater, check with the power company about obtaining an off-peak meter. An off-peak meter allows your heater to operate at times when the company has power to spare, and you may be able to buy electricity at a lower rate.

You can further conserve energy by turning off your water heater if you plan to be away for a few days.

Hot water can cool very quickly as it makes the long trip from the basement to a second-floor bathroom. Consider locating a water heater centrally, perhaps in a small closet in the kitchen. It's also important to have the water heater in a place as warm as is practical. The warmer the environment, the less the water has to be heated.

Locating your dishwasher near your water heater is one way to reduce heat loss, because shorter water lines lose less heat than longer ones.